By John F Bennett

A wartime tale of youthful exuberance, hope, uncertainty and utter despair.

Cover photograph taken by John Bennett in 2023, it is the olive grove where 234 Battery had their positions southwest of Suda bay.

The Letters

Self published by John F Bennett through Amazon KDP 2024. Non Fiction

ISBN 9781399976909

Index

Dedicated to Gladys Bennett nee Garrett, who provided the key to the information contained within this book. Gladys, my mother suffered from post-traumatic stress disorder from an incident during her service in the war. Gladys and two of her fellow radio operators rescued a crew from a fully laden bomber, which crashed near where they were cycling back to their camp after a late evening shift. She didn't speak much about her family or events during the time period I have examined.

However, whilst in hospital in the last stages of her life, she suddenly shook off her shackles and changed from a wizened elderly lady to a person suddenly transported to somewhere in 1941. She was sitting up in bed laughing and bubbly, definitely not the person I had known all my life.

Fortunately, I had the presence of mind to ask all the relevant questions about her brother and other relatives knowing one day I would write their stories. All I had needed was the key which she provided; from there I have been adding to the pieces of the jigsaw to tell their story.

For Mollie and Maisie

Introduction

The Letters tell the story of the correspondence between a father and son during World War 2. Fred Garrett, a WW1 veteran still carrying the war in his head and Aubrey Garrett, his first-born son who joined the Territorial Army in 1936, as the clouds of war were starting to cast shadows across Europe.

Following a consolidation of the family artefacts many of these letters survive, including some from his brother and grandparents.

The Garrett family were bombed out of Folkestone in August 1940, moving initially in with relatives in the hamlet of Bramling near Canterbury, before renting a property directly opposite their temporary home.

Aubrey Garrett had a unique ringside seat to the events unfolding across the channel leading to the evacuation of the British Expeditionary Force from Dunkirk, and then the Battle of Britain. His story takes us to Egypt and on to Crete where he sadly lost his life on 20th May 1941.

None of the letters to the various agencies are in my possession but the majority of the responses survive, indicating the context of his original letters. They give a picture of how a father was frantically searching for his son's last known resting place to finally put his own demons to bed.

All the letters are typed exactly as they are written, please excuse the grammar, spelling and random words. Also, the words used to describe the enemy and foreign nationals in the 1940s would not be appropriate in today's politically correct world, some words are changed to a * but are left in for accuracy.

Where historical events are mentioned, they are not definitive, but merely included to give the reader a taste of what happened in the world at the time of each particular letter.

It has been 79 years since the end of the Second World War and those who were there have diminished in number and soon, they will be gone forever. I hope this book can bring to the reader some of the feelings of that dark period in our history and bring to life a time where every moment was precious.

Foreword

A former Gunner myself who has served 35 years (1984-2020) across Air Defence and Field Gunnery, culminating in two Operational Tours of Afghanistan and finally spending much of my retirement in Crete with an avid interest in the Battle of Crete. I was humbled to be approached to write a foreword for the Author.

Within the annals of John Bennetts' family's history lies the poignant story of Gunner Aubrey Garrett, a tale of unwavering dedication and sacrifice. It unfolds from his military call-up, tracing his journey from basic training through the defence of the UK during the Battle of Britain and culminating in his fateful Battle at Souda Bay, where he now rests beneath the tranquil olive groves of Crete.

Aubrey's odyssey began when he answered the nation's call to arms, a testament to his unwavering courage. From 1937 to 1941, he proudly served in the Territorial Army, embodying the spirit of readiness to defend his homeland, a duty he bore with honour.

The pinnacle of his journey arrived amidst the tumultuous Battle of Crete in 1941. Standing shoulder to shoulder with the valiant soldiers of Right Troop 234 Battery Royal Artillery, he faced the harsh realities of war. It was on the 20 May 1941 that he made the ultimate sacrifice, a sacrifice that symbolises not just his personal valour but also the indomitable camaraderie forged among soldiers in the crucible of conflict.

Amidst the roar of battle, Aubrey's love and respect for family remained enduring. The difficulties of communication during those trying times, primarily through handwritten letters, stand in stark contrast to today's instant connectivity. Each letter bore the weight of longing and hope, a lifeline connecting hearts across the miles.

Aubrey's story also shines a light on the enduring legacy of war—the profound and often hidden wounds that persist. In his era, the understanding and identification of Post Traumatic Stress Disorder (PTSD) were in their infancy, often referred to as "Battle shock." His family's experiences on the battlefield undoubtedly left lasting psychological scars, adding depth to the narrative of sacrifice.

In the serene olive groves of Crete, Aubrey Garrett's final resting place serves as a moving testament to a life of resolute service, a reminder of the price paid for freedom of choice, and a symbol of the enduring love and respect of family that transcends generations. His journey, marked by valour and sacrifice, continues to inspire and serve as a poignant reminder of the sacrifices made by countless heroes in the name of freedom.

'The soldier above all others prays for peace, for it is the soldier who must suffer and bear the deepest wounds and scars of war'. (Douglas MacArthur)

UBIQUE
Lieutenant Colonel Anthony Edwards Royal Artillery (Ret'd)

Chapter One - The early years

The dark clouds of war in Europe crept ominously towards Great Britain, signalling that another conflict was building up steam. No one could have imagined then just how this would turn into the biggest global conflict in human history.

Following the Armistice in 1918, the sanctions imposed on Germany were so strict the country was almost on its knees with poor infrastructure, no means of exporting its goods and limited ability to import food and materiel.

In the 1920 the Socialist Party was formed and the ideals of its leaders gave the population some hope for a better future. The terms of the Armistice set out that the Germans could never again be a threat to the world, the formation of an Army, Airforce and Navy was strictly prohibited

During the late 1920s through to the mid-1930s, the Germans were building their armed forces back up in secret. The biggest threat seemed to be the air force, the Luftwaffe (literal translation meaning air weapon), this was tested and tactics developed during the Spanish Civil War from mid-1936 in plain sight. The tactics learnt in this theatre of war became the standard for the following air war on Czechoslovakia, Poland and England in 1940. On the 18th March 1936, a sixteen-year-old Aubrey Garrett decided to join the Territorial Army at the drill hall in Shellons Street in Folkestone.

Aubrey, together with two of his work colleagues from the Folkestone Gasworks decided to join up. The drill hall was shared by two units training on different nights. They had no idea what units were there and purely by chance Aubrey went along on the night that 234 Field Battery, 59 Royal Field Artillery Regiment were training.

The other unit training at Shellons Street was D Company, 4Th Battalion the Buffs. The Buffs went to annual camp in 1939 and were called up whilst away. They fought bravely in France as part of the British Expeditionary force but always on the back foot, with numerous fighting withdrawals back to the port of Brest when it became apparent France was lost[1].

Unfortunately, the majority of D and C Companies were overrun taking a great many casualties and the remainder, were to spend the next five years in a prisoner of war camp.

234 Battery had 25 pounder field guns left over from the First World war and in June of that year the unit deployed to Salisbury Plain for annual camp. Aubrey had signed on at the age of 16, but was deemed a 'boy soldier' and as such, was unable to complete the basic training until he reached the age of 17.

He was able to join however as a signaller, so did his basic radio training and learnt semaphore during this period. His training on drill nights and one weekend per month continued until September 1937. The unit was redesignated as an Anti-Aircraft Battery with a view to protecting the coastal towns from the ever-increasing air threat from Germany[2].

This didn't sit well with the officers in the unit, they were mostly, apart from the newly commissioned subalterns, old school who had been with the unit since just after WW1, entrenched in field artillery pulled by horses, and as such dressed the part. Even during the height of the Battle of Britain they would be seen strutting about on the gun positions wearing cavalry breeches holding riding crops[3]!

The unit received their first anti-aircraft guns, with a 3-inch calibre and a ranging height of 20,000 feet, and training started in earnest.

These were old war stock and in poor condition, needing quite a bit of ongoing refurbishment. Conversion training started apace to bring the unit to full effectiveness during attending their annual camp at the Royal Artillery gunnery school at Watchet in Somerset shortly after.

On the first of October 1937, Aubrey's unit was re designated as 223 Battery (Kent) Anti-Aircraft Battery under the command of 75 Regiment Royal Artillery[4].

Shortly after the Munich crisis at the end of 1938, the unit was cloned and 234 HAA Battery was reformed under command of the newly embodied 89 Regiment RA. Many of the key personnel went with the new Battery so when Aubrey eventually was transferred to 234 HAA Battery on the 15th September 1940, many of the individuals he knew from the early days in the TA from Folkestone, were already there.

Aubrey was posted to this regiment under the command of legendary officer, Lt Colonel H Stebbings a notable veteran of the first World War, and hero of the 1916 munition explosion in the factory at Uplees near Faversham in Kent[5]. Colonel Stebbings' nephew Peter, was also serving as Aubrey's Gun Control officer.

The basic training for the anti-aircraft units was centred around the use of the guns and their tactics, it was not until Aubrey went to annual camp in 1937 did any form of military training take place. It is also interesting that back in 1937 the issue scales of personal weapons were quite meagre.

The Battery only had two Lewis guns and eight Lee Enfield .303 rifles; half of these were for the protection of the supply routes. The majority of personnel did not have the means to protect themselves. The scaling of weapons was devised in WW1, where artillery units were far behind the front lines, in what was a predominately static war.

At some point the weapon scales increased during 1940, but it only amounted to an extra 4 rifles per Battery! This was particularly relevant in Crete as the scales of weapons remained mostly unchanged, and left the defenders woefully short of the means to protect themselves.

Annual camp was at Weybourne in June 1938 in Norfolk, this would be the first chance they had to fire their guns in training but ammunition was in very short supply. They would have been trained on the old 3-inch guns, but some of the new Vickers 3.7-inch guns were available for the conversion training, albeit it with some critical parts missing.

In 1938 the Government started to call up the anti-aircraft batteries along the south and east coasts for short periods, to test efficiency and put a presence on the ground as a first line of defence against air attack. On the 26th of September Aubrey was called up for full time service for three weeks[6].

In late 1938, the call up had started in earnest but the anti-aircraft units rotated month on and month off so people could still do their jobs. Everyone received a £20 bonus to compensate for lost pay during mobilisation. This continued until late 1939 when all batteries were called up for the duration.

After this he was full time and as the months progressed, other soldiers from regular units and other TA units joined to bring his unit to war establishment, this release scheme then allowed them to return home with the proviso of being called out at short notice via telegram or messenger.

Aubrey only received one call out notice in September 1938, under the rules at the time they could be allowed to return to their jobs under a 'temporary release' scheme and called back at short notice via telegram or a 'Call out Form' as arrived on the 4th June 1939.

67 Warren Road
Folkestone
May 16th 1939

Dear Aubrey,

Thanks for letter received this morning.

I expect you did feel tired on Sunday. Mother and I saw your train go out and the boys were making some row, I bet they didn't feel so much like singing when you got to Watchett. As your train steamed out a young sailor shouted out to someone, you'll be B-Sorry. Have not sent you the Sunday express because there was very little news. Tonight's paper says the first AA units will be called up on June 11th. I saw bombardier Hayden's wife yesterday and she said her husband had written to say it was raining hard when you got there and that it is a one-eyed hole. I understand Minehead is the nearest town. You want to go out and enjoy yourself. I hope the weather is better than we have had it rained hard all last night and it has rained nearly all day and it still looks full of rain. In case you don't know the film for camera is Brownie no 2. If you can't get it there, lets us know and we will send you one and let's know if there is anything else you want. If you get time write and let us know of your doings in camp and don't bring down too many queen bees as they'll be putting another 1/2 d on my fags. Mother has been busy washing today Bill has gone to the pictures with Doug. Must close now to get the post cheerio

Love from all.

Mum and Dad

As a Territorial you had to attend a two-week annual training camp and attend training on a weekly basis for a couple of hours each week. Although it varied, the Territorial soldiers would have to attend for a full weekends training, typically one per month. This rule changed on the lead up to hostilities to two sometimes three weekends per month.

The annual camp for Aubrey's unit in 1939 was at the anti-aircraft training centre at Watchet in Somerset. They would have left behind their guns and gone by troop train, probably a very long day judging by the comments. Troop trains were not given priority and had to pull into sidings to allow the mainline trains to pass, a popular military term 'hurry up and wait' could be applied to this long, slow and tedious journey.

The training school would have its own 3-inch anti-aircraft guns and the crews would have trained in all aspect of their use. Concurrently, they would have refresher training to use the rifles and Lewis guns together with tactics and how to look after themselves in the field.

Watchet was a small port overlooking the Bristol Channel some seven miles from Minehead. The Royal Artillery training camp was located on the hills behind the port with good views of Wales on its forward slopes.

Aubrey's camera went with him while he was in the UK, it is still in the possession of the family complete with an exposed film, no one has dared to open it and try developing it until recently.

The term one eyed hole is an old Kentish derogatory term for describing a place as of poor standard not really fit for habitation, such as an outside toilet or similar building.

Fred refers to Queen Bees in this letter so Aubrey would have discussed in detail what happens at a training camp. Fred would have been interested as he had no experience with the Royal Artillery, as he had been an infantry soldier in the first war. To train anti-aircraft gunners it was common place during the early stages of the war to practise at targets that were being towed. The Queen Bee DH82B was a state-of-the-art radio controlled biplane based on the chassis of a Tiger Moth, using the same engine and running gear[7].

The Queen Bee was brought into service in 1935 specifically to tow targets for the anti-aircraft gunners, it was launched from a catapult and towed a coloured disc. Such was the nature of the configuration they were often hit by the gunners, sometimes as a joke! They could be repaired and reused but the cost to the taxpayer grew as more gunnery training occurred on the build up to the start of the war. This particular camp the gunners of 223 Battery blew a Queen Bee to smithereens!

Fred was concerned that the government would raise the taxes on his cigarettes to cover the cost of new Queen Bee's!

By May 1939 it had become inevitable that we would be once again at war with Germany, the occupation of Czechoslovakia had occurred over the 15/16 March causing consternation in all the European countries.

Concerns had been raised a year earlier when the Sudetenland area which sat on the Polish/Czech borders were annexed by Germany, the reasoning was the area contained more ethnic Germans than ethnic Czechs and Polish citizens.

War preparations continued apace in the UK and by the time Neville Chamberlain gave his infamous 'We are now at War with Germany' broadcast on the BBC[8] on the 3rd September, we had declared war there was no going back now, the future looked very uncertain indeed.

67 Warren Rd
Folkestone

Monday April/May

Dear Aubrey

Hope you are enjoying yourself we have had lovely weather over the week and, have a lot of news for you. We heard from the park's superintendent about a job for old Bill, he went up about it and got the job but it is only for the season but it might help him to get our regular. The job is gardening and the car park Attendant at the tea chalet seven days a week for 35 shillings not bad is it his firm have allowed him to leave to start on Thursday. I am enclosing a letter from Bill.

I had one of my old Cyclist Pals call on me on Saturday, he used to be police corporal and came to Folkestone with his wife to see about a job in Albion Villas and suppose you will be home next Saturday so you will be able to have a rest Whit Sunday and Monday.

I enclose a cutting from the Herald about a recruiting service On Sunday June 4th so you will be in it unless called up for your month.

There was a big air display at Hawkinge on Wed and Sat.

Bill and Dennis went on Sat and they say they had 10,000 people there and understand that the doctor who was to have examined Raymond is away at camp So perhaps he is with your lot.

Well must close Wishing you all the best love from mother and all cheerio.

Mum and Dad.

This was the second letter sent to Aubrey on his annual two-week camp in Somerset. The job mentioned that Bill had secured was at the Little Switzerland tea stall on the way to the Warren at the eastern end of Folkestone. It is interesting it was a seven-day working week in 1939/40!

Fred Garrett joined the Kent Cyclists Battalion in 1914, but was in a reserved occupation so wasn't called up. Only later when his circumstances changed did he join up to go to France[9]. The friend he refers to was a Regimental policeman in the eleventh (Lewisham) battalion of the Royal West Kent's where he served in for the majority of his service.

Initially the anti-aircraft units were called up for a month's duty at a time, with units rotating around the pre-set gun positions protecting ports and vital areas around the whole of the UK. Obviously, the majority were in the south east but the important ports and cities especially London, had a ring of steel around them in prominent positions.

It is also interesting that there were enough guns in storage and training facilities to enable the units to train on their stock of guns in between the call up periods. The old 3inch guns had been in use since World War One. At the outbreak of war there was about 500 of these still available for use, although some were missing vital components.

Hawkinge Aerodrome was to become one of the key airfields in the forthcoming Battle of Britain, some 80 years later you would not know it had ever been there except for a small museum. The airfield is a massive housing estate, with the old officers' mess just a pile of rubble following years of neglect and disrepair.

No one now would have any idea what this little field in Kent had seen and endured in 1940. The only evidence was a permanent presence of the Royal Engineers Bomb disposal section, based there while they dug the footings for the houses. The Luftwaffe dropped thousands of bombs on the airfield and adjacent area hoping to disable the Hurricanes and allow their bombers clear passage to industrial targets.

Raymond was Aubrey's cousin who had applied to join the RAF, I assume he was to have a medical with a military doctor. Fred assumes it would have been the doctor from Aubrey's unit, but in reality, it would have been a RAF doctor based in Chatham attached to the RAF reserve for their own training camp.

The press cutting Fred mentions has survived and is below.

FOLKESTONE, HYTHE AND DISTRICT HERALD, SAT

1,500 Members of Defence Services To March

A.R.P. Recruiting Drive

Drumhead Service At Sports Ground

March Through Streets of The Town

THE most ambitious civic procession yet organised in Folkestone will parade through the streets of the town on the afternoon of Sunday, June 4th, when 1,500 members of the defence services and ex-servicemen's organisations, over 100 vehicles and three bands will make a recruiting march after a drumhead service on the Sports Ground.

A meeting to discuss the march was held at the Town Hall on Monday evening, at which representatives of the local units of the Regular and Territorial Army, the R.A.F., all aspects of Civil Defence, ex-Servicemen's and youth organisations, signified the readiness of their units to co-operate in the event.

THE DELEGATES

The Deputy-Mayor (Councillor R. L. T. Saunders), Chairman of the Air Raid Precautions Committee of the Town Council, presided, and was supported by Councillor E. P. Bridgland (Vice-Chairman, A.R.P. Committee), Mr. G. T. Tayler (National Service Officer), Councillors C. E. Lister and N. O. Baker, and the following representatives of interested bodies: Mrs. U. J. Pain (Auxiliary Territorial Service), Mrs. H. Newkey-Burden (British Red Cross Society), Mr. L. J. Phillips (Boy Scouts' Association), Mr. L. B. Easton (St. John Ambulance Brigade), Mr. G. E. Roden (A.R.P. Transport) Mr. A. S. Beesley (Chief Constable), Mrs. E. M. Weedon (Girl Guides), Flt.-Lieut. L. S. Weedon (R.A.F., Hawkinge and Air Defence Cadets), Mr. E. L. Allman (A.R.P., Decontamination and Demolition), Mr. R. Brockway (Town Clerk's Office), Mr. A. Woods (Fire Services), Mr. H. C. Green (Air Raid Wardens), Mr. W. R. Lyne-Smith (Old Contemptibles' Association) and Mr. E. T. Ames (Royal Naval and Royal Marine Old Comrades' Association).

Councillor Bridgland and Councillor Lister also represented the Folkestone and Sandgate branches of the British Legion respectively.

Welcoming the delegates, the Deputy-Mayor said that, speaking from the point of view of the town's A.R.P., they needed 700 volunteers to fill the gaps. They had tried every way of getting these, and had at last considered that a recruiting march, combined with a drumhead service, would serve the dual purpose of attracting volunteers and assuring the people of Folkestone that the defence services in the town were "in a going condition."

Mr. Tayler then explained the project which he and Mr. Bridgland had offered to organise.

He said that they had already been promised the use of a military band from Shorncliffe and a detachment of 100 troops, a detachment of 50 from the R.A.F. at Hawkinge and probably a band. The service would be arranged by the Revs. C. S. T. Watkins, J. A. Middleton, E. C. Gimblett and J. E. Walters, and amplifiers and microphones had been arranged.

THE BUFFS

Unfortunately The Buffs would be unable to take part as they would be in camp at that date, but the A.A. Battery would be able to march provided that they had not been called up for extra service at that time.

The procession would assemble in Radnor Park and proceed via Cheriton Road, Guildhall Street, Sandgate Road, Castle Hill Avenue and Cheriton Road to the Sports Ground, where the service would be held.

The delegates were asked if they would be able to give their support to the procession, and all were able to reply in the affirmative.

SERVICE BEFORE PROCESSION

Councillor N. O. Baker made a suggestion that the service should be held before the procession; the units could assemble on the Polo Ground, whither they had marched in separate units, and they would be ready to form up in procession after the service.

The matter was debated from every angle for over an hour. Eventually it was decided to carry out Councillor Baker's suggestion.

THE PROGRAMME

The programme was arranged as follows: 2.30 p.m., bodies to assemble on the Polo Ground; 3.0, drumhead service on Cricket Ground; 3.45, procession to move off and march via Cheriton Road, Guildhall Street, Sandgate Road, War Memorial and Leas, disperse in Castle Hill Avenue.

Those members of the A.R.P. services who consider themselves incapable of walking the whole route will be able to ride in one of the 100 private cars which will comprise the transport section of the procession.

A further meeting will be held at the Town Hall on Monday evening, when the programme will be considered in detail, and delegates will be asked to inform the organisers as to the numbers of their parties.

Chapter Two - Going to war, the White Cliffs of Dover.

The inevitable hostilities would see 223 Battery HAA spending their deployment to the east of Dover to protect the port and the Chain Home radar station, the large towers were part of the defence of Great Britain but locally everyone thought they were radio masts.

223 would stay here until they were redeployed to Sheffield and Derby in November 1940, when the German strategy changed to bombing the larger cities and industrial areas, by then they had seen more action than most in the true sense they were on the front line. Dover during this period was nicknamed 'Hellfire Corner'

Further permanent gun emplacements would be built in 1940 all along the cliffs, Aubrey would move to one of these just a couple of hundred yards from their hastily built sandbagged positions, exposed to enemy fire.

67 Warren
Road
Folkestone
19-5-39

Dear Aubrey,

Just a couple of thousand lines to reassure you we no longer have to rely on your measly £1 per week from the gasworks. I had now a situation on the corporation at 35 bob a week. I gave my notice in at Murdochs today. The manager shook hands and cried his eyes out, insisting that I stay on or the firm would go broke, but I up and told him where to get off.

I start Thursday at 10am working all day Sundays. Ginger brought your money around tonight and asked how you were getting on. As I write this, I can hear drunken howls down the road as Dad staggers home from the boozer.

Mum and dad will write Sunday. Hope the weather is finer and the grub good. Seeing as I'm now a man of importance you must raise your hat when you see me. I must close now Dennis wants to go to bed yours until terriers become soldiers.

Bill

PS any communication regarding this letter please write to the Hon. F. M. Garrett. Esquire.

The Garrett estate.

Warrenville.

It is clear in the letters that Aubrey and his brother Bill (actually his name was Frederick but he was nicknamed Bill after a cartoon character of the time, 'Ole Bill in his hole', Bill used to sit in the garden for hours playing in a hole in the ground hence his nickname)

The brothers were straight talking and didn't suffer fools gladly, this was a family trait from the maternal side of the family.

The mention of Bill's dad staggering home from the pub is interesting in the context Bill mentions. His perspective of this was his dad had drunk far too much beer and was coming home happy and singing. The reality of this was somewhat different. I have researched Fred and his early life was full of trauma from the first World War[1]. He had undiagnosed Post Traumatic Stress Disorder, which he suffered from until his death. This burden was carried through his life, sadly nothing seemed to go right for Fred.

He lost his thriving antique shop business due to a random bomb from a Zeppelin, his career as a semi-professional footballer was curtailed due to mustard gas inhalation at the first battle of Ypres. He had a burden to carry, larger than most of his contemporaries.

Fred returning from the pub drunk was a short-term relief, his friends who he served with would all meet up and let their hair down and tell 'war stories' this helped alleviate the pain and mental torture these veterans endured.

Ginger was Aubrey's supervisor from Folkestone Gasworks, who himself would eventually be called up.

The mention of Dennis, his younger school age brother wanting to sleep indicates that the letter writing was obviously well after pub closing time, I suppose this was the only chance Bill had to write after a busy day at work and doing his share of household chores. Clearly, he shared a bedroom with Dennis, leaving his absent brother's room empty assuming he could come home on leave at any time.

The month on, month off call up lasted until August 1939, this enabled the Territorials to continue in their normal employment. That all changed on the 24th August 1939, when 223 HAA Battery assembled in their drill hall at 0800 with all their kit. They may not have realised it then but this was the last day of civilian life for six years[2]. Concurrently, the other units within 75 Regiment, 233 Battery in Dover and 306 Battery in Ashford were doing the same to move to the West of Dover.

A rag tag fleet of 20 hired/commandeered lorries assembled at the drill hall at Shellons Street awaiting the Battery and all of their equipment. At that time, they only had two gun tractors, so they hitched up two of their guns and by early afternoon, they were on the road to a field near to the Chain Home towers above Dover, adjacent to the old colliery overhead railway.

Everything was unloaded and work parties were formed to erect the Boer War era round bell tents, drawn a few days earlier from the supply depot at Thatcham. Concurrently, latrines were dug and work started on filling sandbags with chalk, for fortifying the trenches and the gun pits.

It took about three days to get a normal routine achieved, tasks included digging two deep holes for the command post and the Predictor/Spotters. They had to be quite large in circumference as the predictor needed to five to six men to operate it and four men to crew the height finder.

Aerial photographs taken a few weeks later[3] show clearly the white tents and the seeping chalk spoil from the sandbags around the gun pits.

The remaining guns and any remaining kit were collected from Folkestone the following day, and the key was turned in the lock for the last time.

Over the next few days frantic activity ensued, a trench network was dug around the gun pits and camouflaged. The soil in this area was only three inches deep and then it was down to solid chalk. Hundreds of sandbags were filled and placed as blast defence, definitely not a job the soldiers would have relished, digging with picks and shovels whilst wearing heavy battledress uniforms. Their uniforms must have been filthy and stained almost white with the chalk.

Approximately 200 rounds of ammunition were delivered for each gun in short order, this would need to be hidden from enemy view, the gunners had never seen so much ammunition at one time.

They were fortunate as the weather was good and the field was dry, around the 4th September though, it had rained and was difficult for the group of four guns from another Battery would have struggled to get to their positions adjacent to 223 in the mud, a 3.7 mobile gun weighed over nine tons[4]!

From the middle of October, the weather broke and they soon found themselves sloshing around in ankle deep mud, clearly not a pleasant experience.

Over the next few days, contractors would have arrived with timber to build canteen, cookhouse and accommodation huts, over time Nissan huts would be added adjacent to Upper Road. Some of this timber would have been 'misappropriated' after dark to help with the completion of the trenches around the guns. When the guns were not 'at action' the crews would rest in the trenches and it is human nature to make themselves more comfortable, shelves and an area dug out to use as a table for playing cards was not unusual!

Feeding the troops initially was a problem without field kitchens, arrangements had to be made to feed everyone at the Duke of Yorks Military School which was nearly a mile away. Feeding 300 plus soldiers three times a day wasn't an easy task as the troops had to leave the gun site to walk both ways.

Battery was divided into two sections working a 24 hour shift, the shift started at 8am each day and those off duty maintained the site, did guard duty, unloaded rations, water and ammunition. On top of the down time, they had to cover the meal times for the duty section.

Overall, they didn't get any time off. Some weeks later a further four guns arrived and had to be manned, initially by the existing crews but eventually more gunners from other units arrived and the pressure reduced slightly. It must have been a very tiring time and the Battle of Britain was yet to start!

In these early days the guns would have mostly been manned by skeleton crews for long periods due to the convoluted logistics for feeding and shower facilities.

After a few weeks the tentage would be taken down and the huts would accommodate the whole Battery, this would have been around the end of November much to the relief of the soldiers who stayed mostly clothed during the night until accommodation was useable. They must have been very pleased to break down the old leaky tents.

An officers' mess would have been established and a less grand sergeants' mess. In 1939 unless they were under canvass the officers would have dined in the camp as they would have done in barracks, white table cloths, napkins and Regimental silver would have been laid out for every meal. The whole area eventually would have looked like a traditional army training camp including a guard room, Company offices, Quartermasters stores and ablution blocks.

It wasn't the Ritz quite yet; the electricity and mains water were not installed until around April 1940!

There is now a gap in the letters from late 1939 up to early 1940. I assume that although Fred was very methodical in his correspondence they were lost when they had to move out of Folkestone in a hurry in August. The tone of the missing letters would have continued the theme as before, and likely some amusing exchanges.

For instance, as I mentioned previously, the anti-aircraft gunners would have been trained to hit their targets by a drone, the Queen Bee, but these were only available in the training camps for the Royal Artillery such as Watchet in Somerset. This was too far to travel for the gunners on the cliffs, so a decision was made to move the PAU (Pilotless Aircraft Unit) to Hawkinge to give the gunners some on the job training with the Queen Bees[5].

There was much prevaricating and eventually a decision was taken to move the unit. By this time the gunners were firing at real targets and the PAU was obsolete, they were taking up valuable space at Hawkinge so were transferred back to Watchet in short order.

The invasion of Belgium and Holland began on the 10th May, and bombing began on the French airfields concurrently, on the 12th May the German tanks unexpectantly emerged from the Ardennes Forest and faced the French across the River Meuse.

The deployment of troops was so fast the defenders couldn't keep up with the speed of movement, strongpoints of defence were bypassed and the dash to the Channel coast had begun. The Allied Expeditionary force was divided, eventually falling back to Dunkirk and the remainder to the Normandy coast for extraction via Cherbourg and Dieppe.

The constant manning of the guns was taking a toll on the troops, detachments were being sent to other gun sites, one of note was a whole section including guns went to the Isle of Wight, some went to Hawkinge, others went to the docks at Dover and some to the West of Dover at D1.

Eventually 223 Battery had all its personnel at D2, with the rag tag groups of gunners being returned to their original units.

2nd May 1940

Gnr AC Garrett
No 866845
223/75Th HAA Regt RA
Mount Kemmel
Dover

Dear Mum and Dad,

Just a line to let you know I shan't be home till Monday or Tuesday. As you know I should have come home last Tuesday, but the section suddenly got orders to man two 3" guns on Dover Sea front and of course all leave was stopped.

My name was on orders to go down to Dover but my sergeant has changed gun teams so he went and asked the captain if I could stop as his limber gunner, so I am at good old Swingate.

I expect you will be interested to hear that on Tuesday night a Jerry plane came a few feet over our position in a terrible fog. Our Lewis gun and the Bofor guns opened fire and the lads got the order "take cover" It was a damn good thing they did for pretty soon after showers of shit and shrapnel was descending right on top of our gun pits and huts. A piece hit our chimney and we could hear it striking the road outside our huts.

I wondered if this was the plane that hit a house at Clacton?

The Bofor wallahs say that after they fired the plane flew away with one engine so perhaps, they did hit it

But anyhow cheerio till Monday
Aubrey

The shrapnel mentioned is most likely either from their own guns or the adjacent Bofors guns. The height of explosion is pre-set according to the rangefinder, the shells are made of cast iron with an explosive charge. This detonates at the adjustable pre-set height, shatters the cast iron casing which does the damage to enemy aircraft. It is very crude but extremely effective.

This action was at quite low height with all the surrounding guns firing at the same time, gravity brought down the shrapnel right on top of them. By the time it reached the ground it would still be red hot from the explosion and travelling at terminal velocity, over a hundred miles an hour, extremely lethal for all those without overhead cover.

I suspect everyone in the gun pits was glad they had purloined substantial overhead cover from the contractors when they were building the new camp! Timber and corrugated iron sheets would have been in every gun pit by this point.

The corrugated iron roofs of the accommodation huts were rounded which deflected the shrapnel, had they been flat roofs, then there was a serious danger of injury as the steel was only 12 gauge, easily penetrated by a small steel projectile.

The war diary states that an aircraft flew over at 23.49 hours on the 30th April at 500 feet, the Bofors guns fired 63 rounds but because of the poor visibility the result of the engagement was unknown,

During this period the letters from Aubrey state he was based at Swingate, this was the disused World War One airfield which had been extended and developed as a static army training camp between the wars.

It extended from above the cliffs at Langdon almost back to St Margaret's, it became a significant army camp once the anti-aircraft batteries, heavy and medium, balloon teams, Coastal batteries and Chain Home radar personnel moved in[6].

The aircraft mentioned is probably a mine layer mentioned in the war diaries, it crashed in Clacton causing numerous casualties.

Monday 20 (May)

Gnr AC Garrett
No 866845
223/75Th HAA Regt RA
Mount Kemmel
Dover

Dear Mum and Dad,

Many thanks for the clean washing and Duraglit. I have sent the old washing to the laundry and since it is paid for by the Battery there is no point in sending it home.

I have just finished 48 hours excused duty because I have just been inoculated.

I had two injections and except for a little stiffness, I never felt it at all. They only allow ten of us to be done at a time because the guns have to be kept in action.

We have had no more firing since I last wrote to you last time but we haven't given up hope because several Jerries have been quite close. Last night for instance, they attacked a refugee ship in the channel and the bomb explosions rocked our huts.

This afternoon fifty planes (Blenheim's and Hurricanes) went over and fifty came back. As I am writing another thirty Blenheim's are just coming back. Now the Jerries are so close they take very little time to get their and back.

A fellow has just dropped into our dugout to say he believes that 4 ½ hours leave is starting. I suppose if it's true it is better than nothing.

Every time there is an alarm now, we put out outposts and pickets, all armed for defence against parachute attack. Perhaps Bill and Dad will soon be 'Para shooters' and like our outposts will strut about with revolvers and rifles, and haversacks of ammo.

Well goodbye for now
Yours
Aubrey

P.S. I have just heard the 4 1/2 hours leave starts tomorrow but we are only allowed to go down to Dover. But perhaps it will get longer later. I have enclosed a ten bob note because I will expect I shall want a few things from time to time and this will help to pay for them.

It seems the unit had still been in annual camp mode until the receipt of this letter. The routine of a war footing had not yet been established fully, so the soldiers in the unit were still thinking as civilians. The sending home of washing by post, wrapped in brown paper and tied with string was commonplace with the TA units of the time.

It was only when they went to a war footing did the administration of the Battery pick up the cost of laundry and source the facilities locally.

Duraglit is a tin of wadding soaked in a liquid polish. It is used to clean brass, the uniforms of the time had solid brass buckles and buttons. The standard polish applied with a cloth left a pink coloured residue on the uniform. Duraglit was a much better option as the wadding was reusable and much cleaner. It is still available today and cleans brass just as well.

Military inoculations are still the same today, they don't tell you what they are for and they always hurt! Because they gave Aubrey two days without duty, they were some known reactions to them. The War Diary suggests this started on the 25th April and was for TAB (Typhoid and Paratyphoid strains) and T.T (Tetanus)

It is interesting that a paper was written by the British Medical Association in 1940 on the effects of the vaccine. It states that those who decline the vaccine are seventeen times more likely to contract the illness. This of course is totally irrelevant as no soldier declined the vaccine, they were ordered to comply so any increase in the disease wouldn't have happened[7]!

The rumours and counter rumours here being discussed in the troop positions, started of course by a soldier half overhearing officers chatting, the truth was that as the situation became worse, reinforcements would be leaving Dover daily, and air sorties in support of the defenders would have crossed over Dover as the shortest route to the continent.

Aubrey mentions the amounts of friendly aeroplanes which would have gone over his head at a very low altitude before gaining height to exact their attacks on the German positions.

The Bristol Blenheim was a lightly armed small bomber with little fighter defence capability, hence the Hawker Hurricanes assigned to give fighter cover.

Letters from the gun site at Swingate, which was eventually designated D2 on the local authority plans (just east of Dover on the cliffs) would have been delivered to his parents in Folkestone the following morning after posting during 1940.

The postal address for Aubrey's unit during this period was Mount Kemmel, it is unclear why this was building bore this name, there was a place in Flanders fought over in the First World War and may have had significance to a local unit, but its origins are lost in the mists of time.

The building itself was the old Langdon Prison governor's house, it was demolished later in the war following an enemy bombing attack, its site is roughly where the National Trust visitors centre is today, nothing of it remains to indicate the importance of the structure except the footprint and some protruding bricks.

75 Regiment RA had its headquarters there, all mail for the three batteries would come into the orderly room and distributed to the batteries on a daily basis. That system is still in place today!

It is clear even before the evacuation of Dunkirk started on the 26th May, there is talk on an invasion by parachutists.

The unit clearly hadn't seen much action because he laments the lack of enemy planes to shoot at. The impatience of youth combined with the building national fervour, was creating a sense of excitement and impatience was setting in!

Clearly, the view on shipping in the channel and the battles unfolding in France, twenty-six miles between England and France gave the viewer an unparalleled front row seat to one of the biggest events of the 20th Century.

Both Fred and Bill joined the LDV (Local Defence Volunteers) when it was formed on 14th May 1940. This of course would go on to be the Home Guard on 23rd August 1940[8], this is what Aubrey refers to in his last paragraph.

Friday May 31st 1940 *Same Hole*

Dear Mum and Dad,

Thanks very much for the parcel and socks you sent me. I am glad that Dennis is going to be evacuated.

When they start bombing and I expect they will, it will be nice to think he is out of the way.

I think the War Office thinks it quite likely that England we be invaded from the air. We have been told to defend the guns to the last man, and if the enemy looks like capturing them, we are to blow them up. I don't think that we will ever need to though for East Kent must now be alive with guns.

Although they must be fighting like hell just over the water, things have been quiet for the last two or three days up here. The last time we heard the sirens we saw several German planes but they were out of our range. The Navy fired though and we could see the bombs leaving the Jerry planes but they never hit anything.

The B.E.F must have had a tough time in Belgium and it might be difficult to withdraw them. Thousands might get massacred for they are the wrong set of blokes to give in without a fight. Today's paper says there are 8 British divisions there so I don't think it can be the whole British Army that is cut off.

By the way have you heard from Doug lately? I have heard that the Folkestone Buffs have almost been wiped out.

Has Bill heard any more from the parashots? Tell him not to weaken the butt of his hand hook by cutting too many notches in it.

I shall send those photos as soon as I get them.

But cheerio for now,

Aubrey.

In 1939 the Government decided that children in vulnerable areas ought to be evacuated to areas where the war had not reached. This was known as Operation Pied Piper[9], a steady number of children were sent to safe areas in the country and for a significantly increasing number, to other countries in the empire.

Canada, Australia, New Zealand and South Africa were some of the countries willing to take in school age children. The evacuation started slowly but gathered pace when the channel ports in the south of England experienced air raids and cross channel shelling.

After the fall of France, the pace went up a gear but even so, only 50% of school age children were sent to safer places. Schools were requisitioned in many areas for the war effort but this had a knock-on effect. The parents who refused to send the children away found themselves without schools to send their children to be educated.

When the focus of the war changed to bombing London and the major cities there was a rush to increase evacuation. For instance, the majority of children from Kent went to South and Mid Wales and the youngsters from the northern cities went to quiet areas of Derbyshire.

In some cases, with the focus of the war changing meant some children had to be re evacuated because cities in different parts of the country became a target.

Aubrey's youngest brother Dennis was eleven in 1940 and eligible for evacuation from Folkestone. After much soul searching it was decided that he should go.

Dennis ended up on a sheep farm and although he was safe, he didn't like life in the country. He fed lambs by hand and went to the local school. But in reality, everyone spoke Welsh and no effort was made to accommodate the refugees.

Dennis became miserable and hated everything to do with this experience. We discussed this at length in the 1980s. Dennis felt he missed an important part of his education during this period, and struggled to catch up thereafter. He was terribly homesick which didn't diminish, and finally when the war focus changed again, he was allowed to return to Kent.

Folkestone was still off limits, but by then the family had been bombed out of Folkestone and moved to the countryside. Events confirmed the decision for Dennis to be evacuated were entirely justified, an early morning air raid destroyed much of the house and the corner of the property where Dennis and Bill slept was reduced to a pile of rubble.

The research locally from those people still able to remember evacuation generally recall that life slipped back into routine once the children had returned, and probably the only disadvantaged ones were the younger ones approaching five when the evacuation started. They had to wait until they were nearly eight before the schools reopened

Although he had a successful career firstly in the RAF, and then as an Air Traffic Controller becoming the most senior Air Traffic Controller in Croydon Airport before early retirement through ill health.

The evacuation planning undoubtably saved the lives of thousands of children, but for many they held the experience as the worst of their entire lives.

The evacuation of Dunkirk was about to draw to an end at the time of writing this letter. Aubrey would have seen the build-up of 'the little ships'[10] in Dover harbour and the stream of soldiers returning from France arriving in huge numbers. The information drifting down to units would not have revealed the true nature of events.

The photo Aubrey mentioned was taken when the King visited on the 10th April 1940, the unit had a surprise visit from the King, with about an hours' notice. This couldn't have come at a worse time because they were awaiting fresh ammunition as there had been a problem with the rounds or fuses stored on the gun site which rendered the guns useless. Aubrey had his photograph taken with the King, well the back of him, as he manned his gun.

Aubrey and his team had to pretend to be 'at action' and everyone prayed that they would not need to be actually fire at an enemy plane. The local paper took photographs and after speaking to a few soldiers, the air raid alarm sounded and the visitors were shuffled away to safety.

The gun teams were unlucky at site D3 at the nearby Frith farm, their guns had had barrel changes and had repainted, within minutes a raid happened and they had to fire many rounds. When they cleared down, they noticed the paint had all flaked off the recently painted barrels.

A barrel change was not an easy thing to do, specialist gunners received training in this, it was not until late 1942 the REME (Royal Electrical and Mechanical Engineers) was formed who undertook specialist tasks such as changing barrels. The specially trained NCO would have directed operations, a new barrel weighed just over a ton and because they were not issued any form of lifting equipment or cranes, the task was completely manual labour taking a couple of hours of hard work.

The gun of course would be out of action for that time. The barrels would require painting as they came in gunmetal finish which would have shone in sunlight giving an enemy a head start in finding a suitable target!

The artillery ammunition for all the gun positions around Dover was stored in bunkers in the Lydden valley, just over a mile behind the cliffs. This was manned by the Ordnance Corps and transported by the Army Service Corps on daily basis.

The bunker complex is still there within the local army training area, it hasn't changed much in the 80 odd years since it was built, the only changes to the landscape are the removal of the wooden huts which contained the administration and accommodation for the troops based there.

The media were careful with the news stories during this period to keep the true picture from being shared with German intelligence.

Aubrey would have received the battle picture but not in the fine detail. They would have been advised of the fall of Paris and the channel ports, along with significant areas around the beaches of Dunkirk. His friend Doug Culley is mentioned in this letter. He was still serving with D Company 4th Buffs.

His assumption that he was fighting just across the water was ill founded. The Buffs were fighting a withdrawal action much further west and would ultimately be evacuated from Brest after losing 80% of D and C companies[11]. Doug Culley would be among those lucky to get home.

The gun crews would have been on standby for much of this time, resting in the adjacent gun pits when they could. The 24-hour shift system would have seen great competition from the two teams of gunners, those on duty and having the opportunity for a shoot would have created a rivalry from the team on rest and doing camp admin. The weather in the channel was perfect for the evacuation, unseasonal low cloud and misty weather prevailed for all but two days.

I imagine Aubrey standing on the cliffs to the East of Dover taking in the fine day, looking across the channel, they would still have seen palls of smoke coming from Calais and Dunkirk beyond hearing the distant sounds of thunder. In reality he would only have heard distant explosions carried on the breeze, from the camp and gun positions they had a small rise in the on the coast side of their position, albeit they were on 300 yards from the top of the cliffs leading up to the cliff edge.

The thunder of course was from the German artillery sending shock waves resonating on the early summer onshore breeze. This increased as the perimeter collapsed until the port was finally surrendered. The poor weather in the day's prior was fortunate as it curtailed air attack and the mist and fog shielded the fleet lifting the soldiers from the beaches.

Unknown to Aubrey the whole evacuation was masterminded and controlled from the old underground tunnels beneath Dover castle less than a mile away. Rear

Admiral Bertram Ramsay, the formidable Naval officer from WW1, was asked to re-enlist in late 1938 after two years retirement.

Winston Churchill persuaded him to return to active duty and was immediately put in command of the evacuation planning as a 'Plan B', in case our troops had to make a withdrawal from France in the new few years. Without this planning they would never have evacuated so many men, 338,000 approximately, leaving behind some 35,000 mostly French as a rear guard to hold the perimeter[12].

The evacuation was complete on the 4th June with the last surrender of the BEF on the 12th June when the 51 Highland division surrendered at St Valerie[13].

Near Admiral Ramsey's headquarters in the tunnel complex was the GOR (Gun operations room), where all anti-aircraft activity was controlled in the area around Dover and enemy aircraft movement was plotted.

All this of course would have passed Aubrey by, all he and his peer group wanted to do was shoot down 'Jerries'

Sunday 9th (June)

I got Dad's letter and the parcel ok. The sausage rolls were very nice I thought- and so did the mice. They raided the box in the night and wolfed some of them. But I got even with the perishers, I set a trap in the box and this morning all the mice in the neighbourhood are going round in black mourning.

I am glad most of the B.E.F got away from Dunkirk. We had an AA sergeant from the B.E.F to tell us about German tactics. He said that at Abbeville there were 170 German planes in the air at once. German tanks dragging field guns captured at some of the AA batteries at Abbeville. They drove swarms of refugees up close to the gun pits to stop us firing on the tanks.

I have been down to Dover on leave twice. There is some talk of us getting longer leave but it is not official yet. We are not allowed to go to Folkestone and must return to camp if there is an alarm. There were 200 Jerry prisoners in Dover yesterday, they were quartered at the back of our sea front. Some of them were boys of sixteen.

You must send me Dennis's address as soon as you get it so I can write to him. I wonder if he has gone with his women.

But I had better stop now as I can hear the mice patrols are again active on the grub box front.

Cheerio
Aubrey

P.S. Communique: - A reconnaissance party of hostile mice has just penetrated my defences around the grub box strongpoint. They were surprised by my traps however and retreated, leaving one of their number for the sanitary orderly.

This letter demonstrates Aubrey's wicked sense of humour, despite the impending invasion he finds time to write home a humorous letter. It must have been obvious that the after the end of the Dunkirk evacuation five days earlier, they were staring down the binoculars of the enemy as they scanned the horizon for signs of invasion.

There would have been a natural pause in operations whilst the Germans established themselves, they had overstretched their supply lines and needed time to sort out their administration before they could evaluate their next phase. This period of inactivity would not have been felt on the gun positions above Dover, they would have been steeling themselves for a quick invasion.

The practice of sending combat experienced soldiers to units for a briefing still occurs today, I remember in 2001 attending pre-Kosovo deployment training, soldiers from various units and the support arms came to explain what to expect. Following my return, I did this task myself, giving a presentation to our local brigade headquarters.

The insight on tactics and enemy dispositions was a great help and ensured the troops were a little more prepared. You have to consider they were all Territorials, commanded by Territorial officers[14], who mostly had not experienced combat. The senior officers in Regimental headquarters were veterans of WW1 but woefully out of touch by twenty something years.

The comment at the end regarding Dennis and his women is even today, a complete mystery, he would not talk about his time as an evacuee, probably such an awful period in his life he subconsciously blanked it out.

Aubrey must have been frustrated by not being able to go home, but he and his comrades would have frequented the pubs in Dover and nearby St Margaret's to let off steam. The pubs in St Margaret's were probably the best option at that time, St Margaret's had been almost emptied of civilians, and the military personnel from the Royal Marines manning Winnie and Pooh and the gunners from nearby D2 kept them in business according to the History Society of St Margaret's Bay.

Remember, at this stage the war was still in its early stages and this was a huge adventure for the soldiers, many of whom were between 18 and 23, life experiences to date would have been limited. The effect of the phoney war would have a detrimental effect on their mental health and wellbeing, long before the phrase became fashionable.

The comment about the alarm going off would have meant walking back to camp up castle hill, and about a mile and a half along the lower road towards St Margaret's. This is an incredibly steep climb and any alcohol in their systems would have been long gone by the time they checked in at their guardroom!

At some point transport would have been commandeered to make the journey easier, but in the early days the only way was on foot outside of the normal bus timetable.

The sentence about mice would make sense, they were surrounded by fields of wheat and with the fast-approaching harvest, field mice were in the area with abundance, taking advantage of scraps discarded by the soldiers and the kitchen waste.

This is the last letter home before Aubrey was sent on a course, I have walked the gun site extensively and seen the ground where the original deployment was made, the gun pits and the area where the old bell tent camp was erected are long gone, but the base of the old aerial railway still sits in a field of thistles. This area is now owned by the National Trust and preserved for posterity.

Looking west towards Dover, one of the original Chain Home towers still is in existence, although to the casual eye you would not know what the history behind this structure is.

Moving back towards Upper Road on foot, you come across a brush/wooded area this would have been open ground in 1940, but on close inspection you can see why the farmer hasn't returned this to farmland. The whole area is full of concrete bases and some remaining brickworks where the camp was built. The base for the cookhouse, Battery Quartermaster sergeant and the Battery office can be seen using some imagination whilst comparing aerial photographs from 1940 and the area where the messes were located. The undergrowth is quite thick in places, having been untouched since the late1940s.

There is a straight track leading east from the cookhouse, this track has kerbing and a hard surface. There would have been Nissan huts either side for the accommodation, these are long gone but today the track is being used as a measuring station by the RSPB for migratory bird species, the nets extend the whole length of the track[15].

There is a certain irony to what I encountered two thirds of the way along the track, in amongst the buddleia and hazel bushes is a sole apple tree. My visit coincided with the anniversary of the deployment of 223 Battery, there were green and red apples on this tree in abundance, initially I wondered why there was a lone apple tree there, it is an area of arable farmland but then the truth dawned on me.

A soldier walking back to his accommodation hut from the cookhouse would have been eating an apple, they were generally available at lunchtimes as one of the only fruit options needed for a balanced diet, they still were when I served in 2006. This would have been somewhere between September and October as in the 1940s, fruit was eaten in season as no imported fruit was available.

The apple core would have been discarded and eventually a seed would have rooted and the result is there for all to see some 80 plus years later. Could the soldier who threw away the core have been one Aubrey Garrett? Who knows?

Thursday 13th (June)

Dear Mum and Dad,

Thanks very much for your parcel which I am enjoying very much. Just now It is raining, but we have had beautiful hot weather lately and I am quite sunburnt and feeling fine.

Dad's suggestion that you should meet me in Dover must I am afraid, wait awhile, as all leave has again been cancelled. As soon as it starts again, I'll let you know.

We were in action twice on Tuesday night. The Jerry came a lot closer than before and machine gunned the searchlights and Bofor guns. When we opened up, he had a go at us but he was a rotten shot.

I believe the Bofor guns hit him because some of the lads saw him smoking.

The static guns next to us have come in and we shall move in shortly. The concrete walls should keep the bullets off quite nicely.

Don't forget to let me know how Dennis is going on and to send me his address. I expect he likes being a farmer.

By the way, has Bill heard from Douglas lately? I hope he has not been killed or captured as I believe so many of the Buffs are.

Well, I haven't anything else to tell you now so cheerio.

Aubrey

The summer of 1940 was one of the hottest on record, the effects of the sun for the wearers of the traditional battledress must have been so oppressive, they wouldn't have been allowed to remove their tunics whilst on duty, a throwback to the days of Wellington and the Peninsular campaign[16], where there were more casualties for heat related illnesses than to wounds sustained on the field of battle. Aubrey would have made light of the situation in his letter.

The build up of troops across the water would have given the government concerns that an invasion was becoming more and more likely. Measures were taken and defences strengthened. The anti-aircraft gunners on the cliffs above Dover were considered the first line of the defence, so any hint of leave was just not on the cards.

The guns mentioned would be a variant of the Vickers 3.7 inch mobile guns Aubrey was used to, except the base was shortened and bolted to a concrete base, they were identical in every other way.

On one his many visits to Admiral Ramsey's headquarters', Winston Churchill was briefed on the battle situation. One of the shortfalls was the ability to fire on German shipping that was able to pass freely through the Straits of Dover unhindered. The German fleet based in the Baltic ports could get to Brest and the northern ports in France which would present a threat to the integrity of the British defences.

A frustrated Churchill suggested that long range guns should be installed on the cliff top, with the ability to take on the enemy shipping, and enable harassing fire to be brought to the nearest French towns. Displaced 15-inch guns from the battleship HMS King George V battleship were adapted and used. They had a range of just over twenty six miles.

The first two guns were established in St Margaret's Bay between Dover and Deal, nicknamed 'Winnie' after Churchill and the second one 'Pooh' after the eponymous bear in the stories by AA Milne. All along the cliffs from Folkestone to Kingsdown furious building of emplacements and gun site started to happen on a scale not seen since. The ability to build reinforced concrete structures specifically tailored to the type of gun was a civil engineering feat for the period.

When the Wanstone Farm Battery was identified as a site for permanent fortifications, the small camp a hundred yards or so that he lived in would have been a hive of activity, emplacements and bunkers would have been erected in a short time.

Aubrey refers to these concrete walls in his letter. The site they manned since they arrived was a temporary affair, with just sandbagged emplacements with minimal protection from air attack other than the slit trenches all around the camp and gun pits. When D2 was added to the defence plan the long-range guns and more permanent anti-aircraft guns would share the site, the 3.7-inch guns would be placed on a pintle with the ammunition kept in concrete bays instead of limbers all around the guns.

Additional buildings and facilities would be added during the war. Initially, his unit manned them until other units could be brought in to operate them. Eventually there would be eight guns within 300 meters, four static and four mobiles, with the mobiles set out in a horseshoe shape with the command post in the centre towards the rear, a formidable defence line to protect Dover.

The site was developed further and on the southerly side a further naval gun was added nearer to the cliff top in an enormous concrete structure, the site for 'Jane' 100 yards south towards the clifftop. It was nicknamed 'Jane' after the comic character of the time in the Daily Mirror.

Slightly to the east a further gun nicknamed 'Clem' was built it was named after Clement Attlee, the deputy Prime Minister. This emplacement is still hidden through the passage of time and is on private land today. The heavy guns though, were just in the planning stage when Aubrey was based there, the site grew significantly as time progressed.

These concrete walls are still in place dominating the cliff tops partly hidden adorned with weeds and buddleia plants, and 80 years of bushes and brambles without any indication of the action they once saw.

The search light crews were based to the rear of Swingate Camp just to the north of the camp and the Bofors guns were slightly to the east of Swingate Camp. Bofors guns were effectively an auto cannon with the clips of rounds being fed into a slide on the top of the weapon. They were made by an arms manufacturer in Sweden in the 1930s, they had a calibre of either 37 or 40mm depending on the variant. What made them unique for the time was the ability to put 120 rounds a minute in the air to the height of over 23,000 feet. Their derivatives are still in use today as they are such an effective weapon.

Dennis was still unhappy living in Wales on a sheep farm, he missed his family and Aubrey would have written to him whenever he could while he was still stationed in England to help keep his spirits up.

When the Buffs returned to Southampton, they were allowed to write one postcard to parents/families to tell them they were safe and well. It would be some time before they received a letter from Doug Culley. The unit travelled around after evacuation, spending time near Sheffield for refurbishment and getting replacement soldiers. In 1941 Doug transferred to the Royal Engineers and was subsequently lost at sea in the Mediterranean during a submarine attack on the convoys heading towards Malta[17].

67 Warren Road
Folkestone

July 4th 1940

Dear Aubrey,

Just a few lines hoping you are still in the pink.

We had an air raid yesterday and it was 2 1/2 hours before we got the all clear. At intervals we heard AA fire and one we heard three bursts of MG fire and it was one of our fighters shooting down Jerry just over Copt point way. Several people saw it from Warren Rd and saw one jerry jump by parachute. We had another warning this morning but it only lasted twenty minutes. A few minutes after the siren the guns were in active and the shell bursts seemed over the creek Rd and some say they saw six jerries. But nothing was dropped. Mum was up the garden picking peas and she had to make a bolt for home. No bombs were dropped here yesterday but they let go several inland and at Bekesbourne and a Folkestone man was killed and 3 wounded they were working on the defence works.

Bill got a fortnight notice yesterday along with most of the park's staff. He went to the labour exchange this morning with some of his mates and asked about munitions work. They said men were wanted at Birmingham and they agreed to go and he expects to go on Monday. I think he is going to do the right thing don't you for there is no work here that is likely to last long although we don't like to see you all away from home.

There is no more news about evacuation. We had a card from Raymond to day, he is now in Shropshire and asks for your address which Bill has sent him. His address is:

1254106, AC/2 Casey. R, 10 Squad, "B" flight no1 Wing R.A.F station Bridgnorth Shropshire.

Here is the 9 o/c news so will close and finish this tomorrow cheerio.

Friday:

Here we are again. Just before 6 this morning Mum woke me up because there was machine gunfire and it was our plane stuck into a jerry bomber and it was shot down. Gladys saw it go into the sea near Dover Pier. Have you shot any down at your place. Drop us a line when you get time. We had a nice letter from Dennis and he said the lady wasn't very well so he was helping to dust and wash up. He says he feeds the chickens and calves and he has started to milk the cows. He says they laugh at him when he sits on the stool to milk. We heard from Nannie to day she asks about you and would like to hear from you.

Don't forget to ask again about your photo taken with the King. Well cheerio for now as I want to catch the post.

Love from us all

Mum and Dad.

In the days following the evacuation of the army from Dunkirk, random forays of fighters and bombers would try their luck. This was to cause a nuisance and had a poor effect on morale of the population. Dover and Folkestone were usually targeted during this period so the Luftwaffe didn't get tangled up with the RAF until a formal invasion plan was formed.

Fred mentions Copt Point in his letter; this is an area just east of Folkestone. It is a promontory made of chalk which has been a mecca for fossil hunters since the 1800s. These forays were much easier to undertake with the airfields just across the water now in German hands and fully operational, after just a few days. From their home in Warren

Road, Copt Point was just three hundred meters away so they had a grandstand seat.

These nuisance raids were designed to reduce morale but not to damage the ports. They had been identified for the use of the invasion force as part of operation Sea Lion[17], due to commence once the RAF has been obliterated.

The Battle of Britain started in earnest on 10th July 1940[18], the Germans could not mount their sea borne invasion, operation Sea Lion until the RAF had been destroyed, so from now on the anti-aircraft teams were starting to feel the pressure just as much as the fighter pilots.

The raids came in various sizes and at many times through the day. It would have been very tiring as 1940 was a hot summer with very little cloud and rain – perfect for bombing the RAF airfields!

Aubrey would have been under pressure from the heat and tiredness, they would have been manning their guns with no relief during the hours of daylight. Day on day this would have been very tiring and debilitating

It was only after the focus of the attacks changed to London did the Luftwaffe start to bomb the ports at Folkestone and Dover to any effect.

Bill was not 18 until later in 1940 so he couldn't register to join up just yet. The Mobilisation act of 1939 based its call up on age and everyone was given a serial number. When his number came up, he was allowed to join, he wanted to participate in the war effort and a trip to the munitions factories on the midlands seemed an option. Because of his age and intention to join up, he would have been reluctantly turned down.

The bombs that fell on Bekesbourne were probably on the old WW1 aerodrome. Although it was small it carried out an important task, Lysanders flew missions into France for just a few weeks to drop munitions to disrupt the Germans but this was never really effective. The Luftwaffe intelligence would have assumed it was a fighter station as it was so near the coast.

The airfield was defended by infantry, dug in around the perimeter, the airfield did not have any fencing and anyone could walk across unhindered. These works mentioned would have been to improve the defences around the aerodrome would have been part of the defence lines to prevent invasion forces moving inland as part of the stop lines[18]. Anti-tank ditches were dug either side of the railway at Bekesbourne.

For a small airfield this had a massive staffing level, most of the personnel stationed there were quartered in Nissan huts in the fields behind the Oast houses in Ickham, two miles away. This also had a small landing strip left over from WW1, seen clearly on 1940 aerial photographs. After June 1940, the airfield and its surrounding satellites were abandoned except for a small guard.

Bekesbourne airfield had another satellite landing strip about a mile away just outside Bramling, just in case the main runway was put out of use. In 1943 a crippled American B17 crash landed in the vicinity of this improvised airstrip, the pilot would have thought it could have been a safer bet than crash landing in open fields[19].

As I mentioned earlier, King George VI visited the gun site at Swingate and photographs were taken for the national papers for propaganda purposes These photographs were still in existence a few years ago but they have now sadly been lost[20].

A press photo exists with Aubrey in the background and is in the photograph section at the rear of this book. It seems the developed photographs took their time to get down to the troops, this was a morale booster so the hierarchy would have made every effort to get them to the soldiers.

Friday (20th July 1940)

Gnr AC Garrett
No 866845
223/75^{Th} HAA Regt RA
Mount Kemmel
Dover

Dear Bill,

Glad to hear from your palatial mansion on the Sussex coast. Your confidential secretary is doubtless already suffering from writer's cramp signing fabulous cheques on your behalf.

By the way, I am thinking of floating a company for the rearing of tame elephants in Dorset so if you have any spare cash around, I can sell you a few million shares.

I got 24 hours leave on Wednesday and went home. Needless to say, I upheld the centuries old Garrett tradition of being found drunk in the gutter. On Wednesday night I was honourably installed as a Grand Drinker of the Ancient Order of Pub Crawlers.

We have been in action twice today. They dropped thirty bombs on the harbour but never hit anything. At least one came down.

I see you have now been promoted to a wire bender. How many stripes does a wire bender wear?

But I am afraid that time and tide and Old Hitler waits for no man so cheerio for now

Yours-
Aubrey.

When the Air raid Sirens so who is the first to reach the shelter – Jesse Owens or you?

This letter was sent to Aubrey's brother Bill, but having read it several times and searched the boxes of papers I am unable to work out why Bill was in East Sussex, he had not yet signed on to the RAF so it appears a mystery. One could conclude it was a pre training test as he would sign on to be a specialist and passed the aptitude tests? An alternative idea was perhaps he obtained a job as a gardener for a period of time.

The constant strain of fear and worry whilst being a front line soldier was debilitating, just a few hours at home could make all the difference to a young lad cash rich and an evening out in the pubs of Folkestone, was exactly what Aubrey needed. The paymaster no doubt had paid him his outstanding wages. He would catch up with his old work mates and friends, staggering home elated without a thought of what tomorrow would bring.

At some point Aubrey would have bumped into his father, as Fred was a regular visitor to the ale houses of Folkestone on a Friday night!

Jesse Owens was an American sprinter who had success at the Olympic games in Berlin 1936[21].

Envelope dated 2 August 1940　　　　　*Same old Battlefield,*

Dear Mum,

Sorry I was not able to get home on Thursday, they decided to send us back on Friday and leave was stopped.

Seven days leave is starting on Tuesday. I think I go the ninth week.

I won 2s in the sports for being 2nd in the 100yds.

I have just wrote a letter to Dennis.

Cheerio for now but I will write more later.

This letter shows the importance of leave for the soldiers, they were geared up for some down time but with all thing's army, it was subject to change at very short notice. Aubrey would not see his leave on week nine as he would have been posted to 234 Battery on the 16th September.

Sports and fitness training were very important to the soldiers for morale and to keep them occupied in the frequent period of inactivity. There was also a hidden reason, keeping the soldiers fit and healthy was so important, many of the leaders would still remember the inactivity of the trench warfare a generation earlier. Illness and lethargy were commonplace back in the first war.

The area around the gun sites was grass fields, so ideal for holding a sports day within easy reach of the guns.

Dennis was still living on a farm in Wales at this time, he was incredibly homesick for his family being the youngest of four, he missed his siblings terribly. He didn't return home until the end of 1941.

Postmark 9th August 1940
Thursday

Dear Mum and Dad,

Thanks for your letter, you are right about the balloons, we have 25 around us. Or rather had 25, for this morning swarms of Messerschmitt's came over and shot down 2 of them- 1 in the next field to us. They came so swift we had no chance to fire at them.

Leave is going on as usual and I shall be home on Sunday. There have been 3 civilian air raid alarms today so I suppose you have been very busy in Folkestone too. I'm afraid I've no more to tell you so hoping to see you Sunday.

Cheerio,
Aubrey

By the way they have already renewed those two balloons

Barrage balloons became a frequent deterrent to enemy aircraft, the cables supporting them were one inch thick and could sever the wing of an aeroplane clean off if they came into contact with them. Whilst flying at 200 mile per hour you would not be able to pick them up until it was far too late. Aircraft had to fly higher than was practical for low level bombing and strafing. Pilots were always wary of balloons.

The maximum height the balloons could be used was 5000 feet so giving the targets on the ground breathing space and enable the anti-aircraft guns to engage the targets. On such a big balloon site spares would be kept boxed and ready for deployment for this very reason. The enemy were keen to take them down to allow a safer passage.

When Aubrey's sister Gladys joined the WAAF[22] she was posted to a balloon section. She eventually commanded a balloon site as a corporal on the river Clyde protecting the incoming American troop ships in 1943.

After the war the winding equipment was used to launch the Air Training Corps gliders, one of these machines was at RAF Manston up until the late 1970s where the author learnt to fly gliders as an Air Cadet. It was painted bright yellow but if you looked carefully, you could see the old green WW2 paint underneath!

Postmark 13 August 1940

Dear Mum and Dad

Sorry I did not write to you last night as promised but we were busy all day. In the evening they gave Manston a hell of a bombing but we got at least one when they came back.

I think they bombed Lympe and Hawkinge too and we heard that 38 bombs had fallen on Folkestone.

When I came back on Monday the coastal batteries were firing at something. I think the guns on the East Cliff were firing too.

Well, I've nothing more to tell you now so cheerio for now.

Yours

Aubrey

If you stand on the road by the old Swingate airfield and look inland, the airfield at Manston is clearly visible, so any aircraft flying above there would be targeted on their return to France.

The coastal batteries, nicknamed Jane, Clem, Winnie and Pooh[23] were probably firing at German Naval vessels making an evening dash to open water.

There was some confusion on this day as it was the first time the guns in France fired at Dover, some of the 'bangs' they heard were in fact high explosive shells falling on the town. Lympne was a grass airfield on the plain above West Hythe.

Postcard postmarked 17th August

Dear Mum,
Have been bombed and machine gunned but am quite safe and knocking them down like flies
Hope to be home on Monday
Cheerio
Aubrey

Aubrey felt the need to send his mother a postcard to confirm he was well and unharmed. This experience would have shaken him up, but it wasn't the 'done thing' to show fear and uncertainty. The postcard was more for his own benefit than to reassure his mum! Remember, these lads were only about 20 years old, none had been exposed to the realities of war, their war was fought at twenty thousand feet removing any element of contact with the enemy.

I visualise his Battery Sergeant Major going round the gun pits saying 'right lads drop a postcard off to your parents'; tell them you are fine!

One of his friends in the next gun pit was killed from a low-level Messerschmitt BF109 strafing at tree top level. Shrapnel from the cannon ammunition hit him in the face, he died whilst being taken to the medical officer. This was the first of his friends to be killed, a shock to see the first one and others subsequently would not have seemed such a blow.

Postcard postmarked 26 August 1940

Dear Mum,

Heard that Folkestone has been bombed again so hope you are O.K. Will be home on Wednesday.

Yours
Aubrey

On the night of 26th August, there was a large air raid on Folkestone Harbour which spilled over to Harbour Way,

Warren Road and the adjacent streets. The letters for that period are missing for obvious reasons. One of the bombs went down the coal hatch of 67 Warren Road and the subsequent explosion damaged the house beyond repair. Fortunately, the family were all in the Anderson shelter at the bottom of the garden and were unharmed

The family took what they could carry and moved to the village of Bramling, south east of Canterbury. Aubrey's mother's parents lived in White Cottage, fortunately it was five-bedroom house with only her parents and sister and two brothers living there at that time.

I suppose at that time they thought they would eventually move back to Folkestone but of course that was not to be.

The letters to Aubrey resumed but with no reference to the circumstances of the move and loss of the house. The stoicism in the face of conflict was admirable, clearly, they didn't want to worry him so I suspect correspondence was very matter of fact, as if it was an everyday occurrence.

I know White Cottage very well; I was born there in 1957. My parents moved in there in 1951 after they were married.

After some weeks Fred applied for compensation under the Government scheme for those who lost properties as a result of enemy action. After many months of prevarication, the postal order arrived as full and final settlement.

Fred had to send the ownership documents and any proof of bills he had salvaged to the regional Government office. The amount given for the compensation was just one hundred pounds! This was the standard agreed amount for a three-bedroom house[24].

Fred and Rose would never own their own home again.

Crocksyard
Wingham

27.8.40

Dear Aubrey.

Just a letter hoping you are keeping O.K as you seem to have had a rather a nasty time of it, we can hear your guns at times and my goodness I say to mum and Dad " Aubrey is giving them socks", but they are dodgy devils we've had a lot of bombs dropped our way & my goodness I thought my time was up on Saturday it was the worst we've had so far they dropped their bad eggs about a mile away & didn't we know about it.

Poor Auntie Rose we all want her to come out to Grannys but she won't come well I suppose we ought to understand that she doesn't know what to do for the best as they have his uncle to look after.

Well Aubrey their isn't much to say this time and its almost my bedtime this is my fourth letter I've write to Dennis as I thought he would like a letter as I like receiving letters so I am sure he does.

I will close wishing you all the best of luck also your pals as I feel for every poor kid in the forces nowadays.

Mum and Dad send their love.

Yours
Loving cousin
Lily

Aubrey's cousin Lily was someone I had not known about until I found the letters, despite knowing of her parents all my life. It seems Lily (Lilian) was the only daughter of Fred and Dolly Newing, my great aunt Pheobe in her elderly years used to talk about Lily being a bit 'simple'. I had assumed she meant her sister who died at an early age but clearly the Lily in this letter was into her teenage years simply by looking at the handwriting. She was never mentioned by her parents nor other relatives.

I suppose if you measured her against someone during the 21st century she would have appeared on an educational/behavioural spectrum and had the help she needed. Back then Lily would have just had to accept her lot!

I find it very British stiff upper lip where she refers to German bombs as 'bad eggs', enemy aircraft as 'dodgy devils' and the public school phrase 'giving them socks. The propaganda at that time promotes the stoicism needed to survive and overcome all the adversities being thrown at the citizens. Lily must have embraced this with determination.

By the time this letter would have been delivered down to Aubrey, the family would have suffered the trauma of being bombed out of Folkestone, so the suggestion of 'Auntie Rose' (Aubrey's mother) would have already been on her way to White Cottage in Bramling.

3rd September

Dear Mum,

I arrived back at Dover at about half past 11. I hope the bombing near you didn't scare you.

In the afternoon we had quite a bit of firing. Five Messerschmitt's came down near us and none of ours. We saw 1 spitfire take on 10 Jerries and shoot 1 down in flames.

1 Jerry baled out quite near us. 1 wing of his plane was shot off and they say the pilot was burned terribly.

I have got a different job now for I am to be a Gun Position Officers Assistant or G.P.O.A.

On Sunday they are sending me to Gravesend on an 8-day course so I don't expect I will see you for a week or so. I am glad they are sending me as there are more prospects than being a limber gunner.

I enclose a letter I got from Lily as I think it will amuse you. Let's hope Dad and Bill soon find a job. I will write more when I get to Gravesend so

Cheerio for now
Aubrey

In this letter Aubrey indicates he returned to Swingate at 11:30 am after a few hours at home, I have investigated the transport available in 1940, I was surprised that a regular bus service, the number 90 was available from Folkestone to Dover, and from the bus station the number 80 would run to Deal. It used the main road so hopping off adjacent to Swingate would have made quite a walk to their camp.

Buses ran approximately every twenty five to thirty minutes. Initially it seemed to the author that was quite a significant amount but of course in 1940 car ownership was low together with petrol rationing, bus and train travel was used to the full!

Another possibility would have been those buses and or trucks, could have been commandeered and used to transport soldiers and goods up to the ever-growing camp complex on top of the cliffs. A bus at peak times where soldiers travelled could have been based at the train station and bus garage in Pencester Road[25].

Things were getting serious that afternoon, the bombing that day resulted in the destruction of most of Warren Road including no 67. The excitement of taking on the enemy for these young men was electric. Seeing the result of their work up close must have generated some war stories, the next time they had a few hours off in the pubs in Dover.

Aubrey would have been chosen as the Gun Position Officers Assistant due to his will do attitude. It is likely that he would have been promoted to Lance Bombardier after some practical experience in the role but events unfolded differently.

As the officers' assistant he would have been trained to use the radio building on his previous experience as a signaller, take messages on the field telephone and run errands. He would also convey the officer's orders to the gun pits, so it was definitely a job with prospects.

The limber gunner role he was already undertaking amounted to setting the charges, passing the ammunition to the loader, and being responsible for keeping the limber in good working order and fully stocked with ammunition.

The toll of being alert for hours on end during a hot summer would have been almost unbearable, the lack of shade around the gun pits meant the sun was unrelenting. During the war double summertime was imposed[2] so best use of the daylight was made.

Aubrey and his friends could not have known how the situation was on a knife edge, the RAF pilots were tired after unrelenting sorties, interspersed with the hours sitting at dispersal waiting for the call to scramble.

No 866845 Gnr A. Garrett
28 Bde. School
North Bottom Camp
Nr. Gravesend

Monday

Hut No.1.

Dear Mum and Dad,

Well, here I am near Gravesend on my G.P.O.A's course. I came with another fellow on Saturday afternoon, and we are here for 7 days. There are a lot of subjects on our course including shouting drill. After an hour of this I am quite hoarse. We work from nine to five and we can get out every evening. It is only ten minutes' walk to Gravesend.

I have seen a couple of the instructors before so it is quite like old times especially as quite a few of our lads are up here on a foot and arms drill course.

Don't bother to write to me here as I shall be gone before I receive it. Hoping you are quite O.K and not seeing much of Jerry

Yours
Aubrey

This was a fleeting visit to 28 Brigade Artillery School for his GPOA course. He passed with flying colours and then went back to Dover to put into practice what he had learnt and to get 'on the job' training. Although it was necessary for soldiers to attend career courses, the rotation of leave was very important for morale, so courses were often shortened so the maximum number of soldiers could be on site manning the guns.

The GPOA would stand at the entrance to the command post relaying orders via a megaphone to the gun crews so the ability to shout was essential. As equipment became more accessible did a tannoy system became available but this was long after Aubrey sailed for North Africa.

Chapter Three – Preparations for overseas deployment

On the 16th September Aubrey was posted to 234 HAA Battery just 4 days after his course, the headquarters was at the old TA centre in Sittingbourne under command of 89 HAA Regiment. From what I can gather a trawl of soldiers with certain skills was conducted from other units to bring 234 HAA Battery up to strength with the necessary experienced personnel.

223 HAA Battery had constantly been in action since April, with the intensity building during the Battle of Britain. 223 had the highest score of all the Batteries along the coast due to the 'on the job training' they received, and being in a direct line for the route to the airfields of Kent.

Aubrey joined 234 Field Battery in 1937 when it was a field artillery unit, much had changed when he arrived in 1940, the gunners had done sterling work protecting Chatham dockyard and the surrounding Medway towns, many of his friends from Folkestone were already there so he settled in very quickly. 89 Regiment had been earmarked for overseas service several months earlier, so it made complete sense to have the best trained soldiers amongst its number.

It was obvious that now the Battle of Britain has subsided the Battery was somewhat underused, they were needed in Egypt as the threat from the Italians and Germans in that area could put pressure on the much needed oil fields for the allies.

The war effort was increasing on a daily basis and by now it was clear that the need to occupy North Africa was high on the agenda for the Axis Forces. 89 Regiment was going to be airfield defence for the numerous airfields being built around the areas where allied forces were building up. Alexandria was a critical port to the allied forces in the Middle East which need protecting from enemy aircraft by a 'ring of steel'.

As with all thing's army, nothing gets done quickly in the initial stages, eventually they were given a target date of 29th November to be ready to deploy abroad. The build up to this would have been frantic behind the scenes but to the ordinary gunner, not much would be seen on their level. This would give the impression of 'not having much to do', but in reality, the sheer amount of paperwork, orders, counter orders and draft planning would have been going on til late every night.

Once they were identified for overseas service their priority for ordering replacement equipment would have increased to the highest level, all their guns and peripheral equipment would have been in the best possible condition.

The supply system was split into priority of need, for instance operational units were on the highest state with units such as training schools being the lowest priority, the supply system is still mostly the same today. I imagine if anything was broken or damaged while in the Middle East, the obtaining of spare parts would have been a very long process indeed.

Tuesday *(around 17th Sept)* *234/89th A.A Regt R.A*
Drill hall
Crown Quay Lane
Sittingbourne
Kent

Dear Mum and Dad.

Just a line to let you know I have arrived at Rainham which is about three miles from Sittingbourne. As we came through Adisham on the railway I could see Grannies house.

As far as we know we are going to Egypt but nobody knows when.

We came on Monday and as yet have done nothing. We can go out every night, Sittingbourne, Gillingham and Chatham being quite near.

The Regiment is composed of the old 59th Field Brigade and as you can see, I have gone back to the 234th Bty which I joined up in.

The food is very good and nobody seems to do much. There are guns here but we do not man them.

Well cheerio for now but will write more when we get to know something definite.

Give my love to everybody.

Yours

Aubrey

223 Battery HAA RA, was cloned and 234 Battery was formed in 1938, they acquitted themselves well defending the dockyard at Chatham but now they were withdrawn to rest and reform. The practise of sending a whole gun team would have helped the newly trained recruits and transferees to get trained as quickly as possible. An example of this would be a 'loader' he would have been working his gun putting the ammunition into the breech for months under

field conditions, he knew every inch of his charge and its foibles and anomalies.

This information from someone who had been on the front line was so important when training new recruits, confidence building for one thing, he would have been cool as a cucumber, unflustered and would have given a positive attitude to the youngsters.

The reference to be able to see Grannies house would have been incorrect. Aubrey would have been mistaken, Grannies house in Bramling was in a dip. The houses that he would have seen would have been the cottages at Garrington Farm about a mile west of Bramling.

If he had looked to his left at that point, he would have seen the defence works at Bekesbourne aerodrome, a prewar airfield now being fortified. The Lysander squadrons that initially based there were used to drop SOE operatives into Northern France later in the war[1], but that is a story for another book!

The Regiment was preparing for movement to the Middle East. Whilst the troops were doing low level training the management team would have been working furiously in the background arranging the movement and the associated logistics. The gunners who had been protecting the river Medway would be having some down time, Aubrey would have joined at this moment and found it strange with so little to do after the months of frenetic activity.

The TA centre in Sittingbourne was the Regimental headquarters and as such had more space and facilities. It was formerly the headquarters of E Company the 4th Battalion the Buffs but they were long deployed following the Dunkirk withdrawal. There would have been a fully fitted kitchen on site and the Regimental chefs in situ, so Aubrey would have been well fed!

Prior to their arrival the site was occupied by another Battery who would have manned the guns, but these guns were now allocated to the Battery for use abroad and would need to be serviced and components changed. The 3.7-inch mobile guns were sitting on a four-wheel chassis to enable them to be towed by a Morris gun tractor[2].

All this equipment needed to be in tip top condition because the ability to get spare parts on the other side of the world was a true test of the logistic capabilities at that time.

234 Battery was transitioning through 59 Brigade, it would shortly come under 89 Regiment HAA RA, together with 205 and 235 Batteries. The whole Regiment was due for deployment abroad as will come apparent further on.

Friday

No 866845 Gnr AC Garrett
234/89th A.A Regt R.A
Drill hall
Crown Quay Lane
Sittingbourne
Kent

Dear Mum and Dad

Thanks very much for your letter, since I wrote you last, we have moved to a place called Scrapsgate on the Isle of Sheppey. It is a twopenny bus ride to Sheerness.

We have been measured for tropical kit and we have had several kit inspections so I suppose they are thinking of sending us soon. We shall be glad when we go and are able to go into action with some guns. We don't mind if they give us catapults up here, we hardly know there is a war on.

Give my love to all at home.

Aubrey

Aubrey was clearly getting bored, after the high intensity operations on the cliffs above Dover was relentless for weeks, but being posted and withdrawn to a reserve and training role must have seemed very flat. The adrenaline would have been flowing for many weeks which get the soldiers fighting fit, but in this new role they became a bit drained and the tiredness set in.

The 24 hour, full on intensity of the previous months took a toll on all the gunners, they had worked flat out on full adrenaline levels, they were well overdue rest and leave. It is interesting that they became a bit depressed, listless and developed physical illnesses such as stomach problems. In severe cases some would have experienced a form of what we know today as Post Traumatic Stress Disorder[3], they would have had to shake themselves down, an aspirin from the Medical Officer was all they received.

The frustration shows in his last paragraph, they were chomping at the bit to get back into action. The unit had a high score and this gave everyone confidence and self-belief. The guns were useable but no enemy aircraft came within range. The focus of the enemy had changed. When the bombing of night London became the target, the route in and out of there didn't cross the Isle of Sheppey. The guns at Twydall protecting the docks at Chatham would have seen some action but 234 was now getting an unplanned rest.

Monday 7th

Dear Mum and Dad,

I got back Ok on Friday. We are moving from here this week to relieve another Battery for about a fortnight. We shall be glad to get some action again before we forget there is a war on.

I came back on the bus with a sergeant of ours who was working at grannie's house about 4 months before the war. Some of our fellows come from Wingham so they know Brambling fairly well.

Well, I have no more to tell you now but I'll write more when I reach my new position.

Cheerio

Aubrey

Aubrey must have made his first visit to the new family home in late August, letters during this period were going missing in the postal system. Many of the postal workers were signing on for service together with the ones being called up.

Although the postmen were deemed as a reserve occupation, not too many obstacles were put in the way of those who wanted to join. In reality all active postmen during this period were probably all over the age of 45.

The relief of another Battery involved a trip to Birkenhead to relieve one of the units protecting the docks at Liverpool, more on this in a letter further on.

It was quite likely that Aubrey would have met soldiers from around the Bramling area. The unit was a Territorial unit with troops and headquarters all around the local area.

The unit he relieved in Birkenhead was 93 HAA Regiment, local TA unit formed at the same time as Aubrey's.

Undated

No 866845 Gnr AC Garrett
234/89th A.A Regt R.A
Shorefield
New Ferry
Birkenhead
Cheshire

Dear Mum and Dad,

Well as you can see I have arrived in Birkenhead O.K.

We left Sheerness at 8pm on Wednesday and arrived in Birkenhead at 10 next morning. You can guess we are all very tired

We have a beautiful position here on the banks of the Mersey just across the river from Liverpool suitably surrounded by such nonmilitary objectives such as dock yards and oil tanks.

We have a 4.5" gun site and I am on the "Predictor". On our first night we put up a barrage which the papers say got a plane. The lads from Hells Corner know their stuff!

Jerry doesn't seem to penetrate here much in daylight although we have occasionally seen one. It is certainly a change to see a Dornier without a swarm of Messerschmitt fighters round it. The R.A.F have shot down several.

We have a fine view of Liverpool- the Liver building and the Cathedral being very plain. The grub here is fine and it's the best site I have been at.

So far as we know we are here for 10 days. Then I expect we shall return to Scrapsgate.

Well, that's about all I have to tell you now so cheerio

Yours

Aubrey

234 HAA Battery went to Birkenhead to relieve a Battery in need of training and refurbishment. They were taken out of the front line and sent for training. 234, one of the most

experienced and highest scoring batteries protecting the docks at Chatham during the Battle of Britain, spent ten days protecting Liverpool.

For them it must have been a bit of an anti-climax, they had been very busy during the early stages of the Battle of Britain, but incredibly quiet at the gun sites on Sheppey when attacks began to subside. The challenge of getting back in action would have been a relief.

The 4.5-inch guns were familiar to the lads from 223, they had manned them down at the docks at Dover whilst covering leave periods before.

It is interesting to see that Aubrey was working the 'Predictor', it is clear that he was a skilled gunner, having passed the course to be the assistant to the Gun Control Officer, he now was working this incredibly complex piece of equipment. The Kerrison predictor made by Vickers was developed in the 1930's initially to aid Naval gunnery on board ships, but it subsequently proved more efficient than the existing way target acquisition was achieved.

It was effectively a computer, you twisted dials to input the aircraft speed, height and the angle of the gun to the target and it worked out the exact spot the shell would explode after working out the lead time of the projectile.

A simpler device to operate was made by Sperry, it was an incredibly accurate device and very effective on aircraft flying in a straight line although when it was first issued the gunners complained they were hitting less aircraft[4]. They reverted to the old Vickers predictor until the Sperry devices were recalibrated.

Tuesday *(18 Sept 1940)*

No 866845 Gnr AC Garrett
234/89th A.A Regt R.A
Drill hall
Crown Quay Lane
Sittingbourne
Kent

Dear Mum and Dad,
As you can see, we have come back to Scrapsgate again. I was really sorry to leave Birkenhead as we had a splendid time there. Everyone was very kind to us and they seemed much more friendly than in the south.

I was sorry to hear about the air raid in Folkestone. It seems a good job that we moved.

I don't know ~~that~~ if we shall get 24 hours leave here. I think perhaps we will so I may be home again shortly.

Well cheerio
Yours
Aubrey

After the air raid which left the family homeless, Folkestone became a focus of the enemy with bombing raids and cross channel guns pounding the area around the harbour, my view would have been that the threat of Operation Sea Lion[5] had diminished, so the ports closest to the French coast would have been targeted to put them out of action. If there was a counter invasion in the future, these ports would have been used for landing craft etc.

Scrapsgate was an open field on the Isle of Sheppey, not the most hospitable of places, Birkenhead would have seemed a pleasant change being housed in old school buildings, with easy access to local pubs!

Myrtle Cottage
Bramling
Wingham Well
Nr Canterbury.
Thursday 26th September 1940

Dear Aubrey,
We received your letter from Sittingbourne and mother answered it. We have not heard from you since, so perhaps you have moved again. You will see by my address that we have moved home Mum and Glad went to Folkestone last Saturday and packed the things and Bill and I went down on Sunday with a lorry and moved up here we got most of our own stuff and are pretty comfortable we slept here on Tuesday night. The place has been decorated and I think we shall be happy here Gladys finished hopping on Monday and I've finished today the farmer said I can have a job there so I shall stick it and perhaps a better job shall turn later on. Gladys had the chance of a job as a cook at Col Friends but it is to cook for 6 people and she thinks it may be too hard for her but she is going there for a bit until they can get a cook. Bill is still working at Bridge Nanny sent you a cake and a box of chocolates for your birthday but as she has lost your address, she sent it to us to give to you but owing to postal delay it took a fortnight to come we do not know whether to send it onto you in case you had gone away. We all wish you the very best of luck and a speedy return to peace and home love from us all Mum and Dad.

The move mentioned in the letter was in fact this time just across the road, the furniture and the remaining belongings had to be collected from the ruins of the house in Folkestone.

A childhood memory I still hold, is the mismatched and damaged family chattels, odd crockery and cutlery. It was something that had plagued them for years. They had lost their house and business to a rogue bomb from a

Zeppelin in WW1, and had to salvage what they could from the wreckage twice in 30 odd years.

Hopping was a local term for hop picking, Gladys would have found it easy to get a job locally, the whole area was full of hop fields, thirteen[6] in fact all within a short walk or bicycle ride. They would have arrived in Bramling as the harvest was in full swing. Short term labour for the hop season was easy to find before the war and indeed in the post war years, but as most of the workforce came down from London as families to coincide with their annual holidays, the Blitz has discouraged them to leave their homes. Not knowing if they would still be there after 2 weeks would have put most people off.

Local labour in the form of housewives, farmers' wives, children nearing the end of their schooling and those who had retired but still active were the main source of labour for this intense 2 week period.

Gladys would have left her job in Folkestone as the housekeeper to the vicar of St Mary's just down the road from their house in Warren Road, although her post was a live in situation, she didn't want to be away from her family and the threat of constant air raids was a little daunting for a young single girl away from her parents.

Colonel Friend and his family lived in the manor house in Bramling (Bramling House was one of the largest houses in the area with an estate), It was one of the few houses that had its own generator, providing 12-volt electric lighting for the whole house. Latterly, the Friends' moved to Duckpitts farm following a decision to retire in the 1950s. I can confirm though, that Gladys continued to work there as cook and housekeeper until 1957 when I was born.

Tuesday
Oct 1st

Myrtle Cottage
Bramling
Wingham
Nr Canterbury

Dear Aubrey,

We were all pleased to hear from you, your letter was dated Friday I wrote and told you that nannie had sent to us a cake and some chocolate for your birthday, shall we send it onto you we quite thought you had gone as we hadn't heard from you. A picture in todays Daily Express shows some troops disembarking? In tropical kit and mum and Glad were looking through the glass to see if you were amongst them. We are comfortable in our new house Bill is with us he is on the sick list he was hit on the head with a pickaxe last Friday and was taken to hospital by ambulance but thank goodness it was not serious he had it stitched and came home and is going on ok. Mum and Glad went to Canterbury and met Doug on his way to see us. He stayed the night and went back Saturday evening. He is on 7 days leave.

Well old son write as often as you can and don't be afraid to ask for anything you want. Have you got enough money. We all wish you the very best of luck and a speedy return home. So write as often as you can as mum will worry about you. Cheerio and all the best

Love from mum and dad

PS let us know if we shall send on your parcel if not we will send you a parcel when you reach your destination

The glass Fred mentions is a solid silver magnifying glass salvaged from the ruins of the old antique shop in Folkestone, embossed with the words German Silver. I still have it in my possession to this day. As they hadn't heard from Aubrey for a few days his mum, Rose assumed he had gone abroad, such was the lack of understanding of the process on the home front.

Bill had a scar on his hair line visible all his life due to that incident with the pick axe, it appears the axe head flew off and hit him during some rough digging! He was plagued with headaches all his life because of this accident, he became dependant on pain killers and took a nap every afternoon, one day in 1972 he didn't wake up from one of his naps, he had suffered a fatal heart attack.

Approx 3 November 1940

No 866845 Gnr AC Garrett
234/89th A.A Regt R.A
Drill hall
Crown Quay Lane
Sittingbourne
Kent

Dear Mum and Dad,

Just a line to let you know that I got back to Sheerness O.K. About 4 o'clock this afternoon. From Canterbury I got a lift to Sittingbourne with a couple of our fellows I met. We bussed to Sheerness and since I had a return ticket I got back for nothing.

Ive no idea when I shall be home again but Ill let you know

Well
Cheerio for now
Aubrey

A bus to Canterbury from Bramling was an easy means of travel, they were frequent on that route even during wartime, the bus stop was just outside the Volunteer public house about a hundred yards down the hill from their house.

No 866845 Gnr AC Garrett
234/89th A.A Regt R.A
Pathfield road school
Clacton on Sea
Essex

Dear Mum and Dad

As you can see I have arrived at Clacton on Sea. We got in about eight oclock on Monday night practically wet through. We are in a former girls school.

We passed through London on the way up and saw some of the damage all the way along the line.

As far as we know we are here for further training and fitting out though so far ive done nothing.

We have been told that we are to be ready for tropical service by the 29th(November). Most of us are glad that we haven't much longer to wait.

All our Battery is billeted in two schools but the rest of the regiment is in Butlins holiday camp. They tell us they have great thick carpets on the floor.

This is about all that has happened so far but ill let you know what happens

I think we will get more leave soon.

Cheerio
Aubrey.

The Regiment was warned off for mobilisation and be prepared for overseas service[7], on the first of November, all three batteries were instructed to move to Butlins holiday camp in Clacton where they prepared their guns and equipment for the deployment[8].

The guns and limbers would have been covered in heavy grease to prevent air and salt water corrosion, it wouldn't have mattered had the journey been only a couple of days, but this likely time at sea was over 6 weeks. A very dirty job indeed, almost as bad as wiping it off at the other end with the abrasive threat of sand causing almost as much damage!

The Pathfield Road school was divided into separate schools for boys and girls, 234 Battery took over both schools, accommodation was on camp beds in the school hall and classrooms used for lectures and training. It was demolished after the war; Clacton Coastal Academy now stands on the site of the former school.

At some point all the guns and heavy equipment would have been taken to the port of departure Glasgow, probably at least two weeks before sailing for loading onto transport/cargo vessels.

Collective training would also take place, shooting and tactics would have been refreshed, together with equipment checks and fitness training.

The personnel in key roles would practice every aspect of their job on tabletop exercises to ensure everyone knew their jobs.

There would have been various posting in and out of the Regiment, the new intakes would have to integrate and be brought up to the same level of training and fitness.

The Regiment had nearly a month to prepare for oversees service. This seems quite a long time but periods of embarkation leave had to take place. The soldiers would be instructed to take home any kit or personal items. Even cameras were deemed as non essential, letters and most non issue items would be left at home.

Stone Road
Langtoft
Peterborough
Saturday 16th Nov.
Dear Aubrey,

So, you have got your orders to proceed to some foreign clime where it maybe I suppose even you can only conjecture. Well, my boy it will be a fresh experience, giving you an opportunity to view scenery and see customs of other races of people which would not be within your reach as a civilian. When you return you will be able to make your parents and grandparents hair stand on end with your thrilling experiences you will make us all envious relating the wonderful stories you will be able to tell you know the old sweats touch. No doubt you will have good and bad times but this happens every phase of one's life, but I assure you I sincerely hope the good will be predominant. When you are away from good old England don't forget to drop us a few lines because we shall always have you in our minds when you encounter the enemy. If this should be your lot his thin blue pencil hard and show him the same mercy that they would show you and don't let the black women steal your buttons off your uniform. well Au Reviour god speed and pleasant and safe voyage

yours gratuitously Grandfather.

This is the last letter Aubrey received from his grandfather, Charles[9]. Charles clearly had a feeling that tough times were ahead and was trying to reassure Aubrey. He tries to convey that a sense of fairness should be applied to an enemy. Charles was well educated, attending the Willam Harvey Grammar School, in Folkestone in the late 1880s. he didn't serve in the First World War as he was over the age limit, but would have heard the stories of the grim and atrocious conditions by those first hand by his son.

Stone Road
Langtoft
Peterborough
C/o Mrs Sargeant
Stone Road
Langtoft
Peterborough
Sat Nov 16th.

Dear Aubrey,

I had a letter from your Dad today I was glad to hear you had been to see them now we all wish we could see you before you go away. Raymond was very disappointed because he did not see you, I have had a very bad cold and have been quite ill with it. But it is now getting better, is there anything you would like me to send you before you sail if so please let me know and I will send it to you. Do you get good food, you have had plenty of moves you are seeing a bit of the world. I hope that Musso and his gang are mashed up before you have to go. Keep your chin up boy. We will pray for your safe return. I do miss seeing your dear father it breaks my heart to be parted from him or such a long time, it seems years since we came here the time seems so long, I am glad that Bill and Gladys are with your mum and dad that is a great load off my mind it is nice to know they are together. Please god we shall all be together again soon don't forget to let me know what I can send your auntie Glad, send her love to your Grandfather is enclosing you a few lines, now cheer up my boy Fondest love to you from your loving nanny xxx God bless you and keep you safe from harm.

This letter was included in the same envelope as the one from his grandad. It is from Alice, Aubrey's grandmother, somewhat less maudlin than his grandfathers. She mentions

'Musso', he was the Italian Dictator Benito Mussolini, who had designs of empire building in North Africa and Greece.

Monday 18(November)

No 866845
Gnr AC Garrett
234/89th A.A Regt R.A
Butlins Camp
Clacton on Sea
Essex

Dear Mum and Dad,

~~*W*~~ *I received your letter the other day. We are still quartered in the same place though as you can see they have altered the address.*

By the way, Butlins Camp is only about a quarter of an hours walk from here. I have been there twice- once for a bath and once for a concert.

Clacton itself is much like Folkestone, very few civilians are there. When we go to the pictures the place is crowded with troops almost entirely.

There is not much to do here except a few fatigues now and again and I am getting quite efficient at dodging even them. The other day the orderly Sgt was on the warpath for a fatigue party, I made a strategic withdrawal to the canteen, another Sergeant inside said 'hello have a cup of tea' I was only sorry it was not a pub.

The grub here is very good and we get plenty of tea.
We have just drawn most of our tropical kit, you should see me in my toppie or pith helmet.
I am sorry to hear that Jerry has been active near you. We see very little of them here except at night.

I should hang on to the gloves for a while as I might be home. I understand the decision was to send us over without any leave but I believe the officers are appealing against it. I think we shall get a few days.

Give my love to all at home and cheerio for now.

Aubrey

I am assuming that the embarkation date was brought forward and the promised leave was either cancelled or shortened. Leave was eventually given and everyone had five days back with their families before the long sea journey that lay before them. They would have taken home on their final leave all personal things such as cameras and home comforts such as small stoves and camping kettles etc.

Aubrey left his camera with his parents on this final visit, more about this later! No photographs exist of Aubrey wearing his pith helmet, the only ones show him wearing a side cap. Brand new tropical kit although thinner than the standard battledress would have been stiff and uncomfortable with the ubiquitous smell of mothballs, no doubt every one washed theirs within a few days to get rid of the starch and the smell!

Tuesday 26th *No 866845 Gnr AC Garrett*
234/89th A.A Regt R.A
Butlins Camp
Clacton on Sea
Essex

Dear Mum and Dad,

As you can see I arrived back O.K. yesterday. I met young Harvey and we crowded into a small car that already held three. The train was half an hour late and we had to change and wait for another train at Chatham.

We got off at London Bridge and as it was nearly twelve then, we took a taxi to Liverpool street. The perishing thing kept stopping every five yards but when we did get going we went so fast my hair stood on end.

We got into the station as the train was going out and we had to run like hell to get on. Into the carriage that went by I flung my helmet, into the second my parcel, into the next went my overcoat and into the last went me. It took me about threequarters of an hour going along the train to retrieve my belongings.

Well this is about all I have to tell you now so
Cheerio
Aubrey

It seemed that to overcome the change in embarkation indicated in the text of the letter, the whole Regiment went on leave together for five days, leaving only rear party and minimal personnel behind to guard the camp. Aubrey managed to get his train by the skin of his teeth, had he bit late for the reporting time he would have been in trouble. Army regulations were and still are very strict with regards to reporting time coming back from leave!

Dec 12th (Thursday)

No 866845 Gnr AC Garrett
234/89th A.A Regt R.A
Butlins Camp
Clacton on Sea
Essex

Dear Mum and Dad,

I have just received your letter complete with mirror quite O.K. By the way this is the last letter I shall write to you from England as we have just received orders to move and should be at our port of embarkation on Monday(16th).

Once their we shall not be allowed to write or telephone and thus disclose where we are sailing from.

We have been told to prepare for a six week journey so I guess we are going round the Cape. I am to see things are livening up in Egypt and if all goes well we should be in time for our share of socking the Wops.

We have been given a new address (I shall write it on the end), and if you send letters to it they should reach Egypt as soon as ~~they~~ we do.

While I think of it in your first letter will you send me Raymonds address as I have lost it. By the way I have sent you two letters since I came back off leave so evidently one had gone astray. Your letter has taken 3 days to reach here.

I think we shall sail very soon after reaching the port so we shall have Christmas as sea. Perhaps we shant feel like eating anything though.

I heard that my old mob has moved to Sheffield. I also heard that Colonel Sadler of the 75th Regt has received the O.B.E. for shooting down 90 planes. (The Regiment I mean not him).

If it takes us six weeks to get there I suppose it takes six weeks to get a letter back so it will be about 3 months before you hear from me again.

But, once there I will write as often as I can.

I shall write to Dennis before I go and send him a present. I was sorry to hear he has been amongst floods, and that you have had more lambs. Lets hope they keep off for a bit.

I hope everyone at Grans is O.K.and give my love to all. Tell Bill to raise the dead with his mouth organ.

And so best wishes for a happy Christmas and cheerio for now.

Aubrey

The new address is:

No 866845 Gnr AC Garrett
29894 (C)
GHQ 2nd Echelon
C/O Army Post Office 725

Aubrey would have known the port of embarkation was going to be Glasgow, the ships would have been moored all along the relative safety of the river Clyde. Two years later his sister Gladys would be in charge of a balloon section in the same area protecting the incoming American soldiers from random Nazi air attack.

The vehicles, guns and heavy equipment would have taken the arduous road journey north many days earlier, in those days road movement during wartime was complicated with a poor road network, no motorways yet! The remaining soldiers would have been taken by train; this would have been over a 24hr journey. Aubrey's letter is dated 12th December which was a Thursday, so he was well aware of the journey ahead.

Aubrey's old unit 223 HAA Battery, and the rest of 75th Regiment was moved to Sheffield to protect the steel works and factories. The Commanding Officer was rightly awarded an OBE (Order of the British Empire) for the work done during 1940 when his guns were the first line of defence against the German Luftwaffe. 90 aircraft were shot down between July and November, a significant number that would have put a strain on the enemy resources of both aircraft production and training new pilots and crews.

Chapter Four – The journey to Egypt

Friday Dec.27th

No 866845 Gnr A Garrett
29894 (C). GHQ 2nd Echelon
C/O Army P.O. 725

Dear Mum and Dad,

This comes to you from mid ocean to let you know that after a riotous bout of sea sickness I am once more my hale and hearty self. We are ~~k~~now sailing in calm and fair weather and am enjoying to the full the restfull sea cruise bestowed on me by a benevolent Government. Beyond saying we have actually left England I am not allowed to tell you where are or where we are going (even if I knew)

The first four days out I was violently sea sick, so much so that one old sea dog asked if I had a season ticket for my part of the rail. But I was not as bad as some of the others and I soon became quite O.K. ~~until~~ and ~~today~~ when I am regarded as a Mariner second only to Popeye.

I hope you had a fine time at Christmas. Ours was better than we expected to get on such an old tub as ours. When we first saw her even the hardiest of us ~~who~~ were unwilling to risk our lives on such a decrepit crate and there were some who even doubted our ability to reach the three mile limit.

But so far she has refused to sink and we are all easier in mind now that we know for sure she is not 'Sir' Richard Grenvilles flagship "Revenge", as we had at first thought, but the "Altmark," in disguise.

~~By~~ So far this about all that has happened on the voyage but If we get any further ~~oppoti~~ opportunities for sending letters Ill let you know.

Don't forget you can send letters to the address at the top of this letter.

So Cheerio for now,

Yours,
Aubrey.

Don't let Bill or Raymond know I was sea sick or they/ll harp on it for years.

A Corbett 2lt (censor)

The ship that transported the unit plus others from Glasgow to Port Tewfik in Suez, was HM Transport ship T5, the TS Canterbury. This ship was owned by Southern Railway before the start of the war. It was exclusively used a 'boat train' when the railway used to speed up the journey from Paris to London before it was requisitioned in early 1940.

The capacity of this vessel was probably about 600 but, on this journey, it carried 49 officers and 1419 men (albeit they lost a few to absence when they reached their destination after a night out in Durban!)

Who could have imagined where this small steamer would have taken troops during the war, it was built to hop across the English Channel eight times per day from Folkestone. I wonder if Aubrey recognised it as he spent quite a bit of time in Folkestone harbour before the war? That sense of 'oh my goodness' when he first set eyes on the familiar vessel.

It took part in the evacuation from Dunkirk, saw the equator several times and rounded the Cape of Good Hope, went to the Far East, and she crops up on D Day +2, transporting troops to Normandy. Not bad for a tiny vessel!

The route taken would have subjected the convoy to the rough and violent seas to the west of Ireland, with all that the winter could throw at it. Seasickness must have affected nearly everyone. This vessel would have been one of the smallest in the convoy.

It's strange that Aubrey states that the ship is an 'old tub' and a 'decrepit crate'. The vessel was only eleven years old! Evidently the cause of the soldier's illness and upset stomachs were directed in the direction of their transport.

The German ship 'Altmark' was in the news in early 1940 during the events in Norway. The Altmark was a German resupply ship that shadowed the heavy cruiser Admiral Graf Spee. When the Graf Spee attacked allied merchant vessels in the Atlantic, the crews were transferred to the Altmark as prisoners of war. The Graf Spee was scuttled in Montevideo harbour following a successful British Naval action which seriously damaged the ship. The Altmark made for home port but became low on fuel and headed to the then neutral Norway.

On the 16th February 1940 she was spotted by an RAF reconnaissance aircraft and through the determination of the Prime Minister to obtain a morale boost for the British people, wished to free the British sailors. The Altmark was cornered in a fiord by HMS Cossack on the 17th February and after a short exchange of fire, the Royal Navy boarded the vessel.

Rumours still abound that the crew used old fashioned Naval cutlasses to frighten the Kriegsmarine sailors. When the ship was searched the Navy found 299 prisoners who were taken back to UK port. The Germans suffered four sailors killed in the altercation with no allied casualties.

Because Norway was then a neutral country, the Altmark was allowed to continue its journey. It is said the Adolf Hitler changed his view on neutral Norway after this incident, at that time they were importing steel from Sweden which was transported to the sea ports in Norway for onward movement to Germany. Norway was next on his list for occupation to safeguard the economic route.

The news of the prisoner rescue was a tremendous morale boost at that time, rationing, blackouts and control of movement in the UK were taking their toll. The news of the rescue gave some sort of justification that actually something was happening positively in the war to date[1].

Myrtle Cottage
Bramling
Wingham
Nr Canterbury
Sunday

Dec 29th 1940

Dear Aubrey

Here we are again, all of us ok and we hope you are fit and well. We have no doubt now that you are on the sea on your way out east and we hope and pray you will have an uneventful journey and arrive safely at your destination.

Well old son xmas is over and we hope you had a good time. It was quiet here and our thoughts were with you, Dennis and Nanny. We had a good dinner of tame rabbit and pork and with a pudding that granny gave us. The rabbit Bill won in a raffle when he went to Wingham to see Sid, so our luck was in. Xmas afternoon Gladys and Bill went to uncle Fred's to tea and mum and I went up to granny's. It really didn't seem a bit like xmas. We had a parcel from Dennis which had a present for all of us.

There were handkerchiefs for mum and Gladys a tie for Bill, two sticks of shaving soap for me and for you he sent a wallet with writing paper and envelopes and he asked to send it onto you which we will do later on.

We had a letter from Raymond who was home for 7 days at xmas, he is now with the barrage balloons that he says he likes better than the police. I had xmas and Boxing Day off with pay but Bill had to work on Boxing Day but he will get double pay for it.

By the way Dennis was delighted with his registered letter enclosing 5/= that you Kindly sent him.

Bill sent him 2/6 and we sent some books again a pyjama suit, a pair of gloves and some sweets and granny also sent him a parcel so he didn't do too bad. We haven't heard yet how he spent xmas but he said they had made eight puddings they were lucky for most people couldn't get any fruit to make a pudding with.

We couldn't get any oranges we got a pound of brazils[2]and a pound of Apples and granny gave us a bottle of cherry wine. Of course I managed to get a few pints along the volunteer. Doug Culley was home for 7 days leave and had to go back just before xmas he came up to us and stayed a night and Bill went down to him on the Sunday. Bill said our old town is badly knocked about in places uncle berts house is down to the ground but we don't know if anyone was hurt.

Young Raynsford came out to tea the other Sunday and he said where his fathers shop stood is now only a crater and everything was lost. The Royal George pub was so badly damaged that is collapsed we have had it fairly quiet as regards to raids over xmas there was nothing doing, but this last few nights the night raids have been thumping? over we are giving old Musso something to get on with and we hope we can finish him off before you get into the action, I hope jerry Doesn't go to musso's help. We wonder what sort of a sailor you are making and how you are enjoying your sea voyage I expect they gave you a good xmas dinner and we hope you were not like the chaps on the wireless who said he had 2 dinners 1 down and 1 up. We have not much news for you but from now on I will write to you at least once a week and give you what news there is I expect we shall have to wait a long time before we hear from you. I saw Mr Harvey on Saturday and he said they had a letter from his son which said he was on a well known ship and hoped to make a good sailor the letter was censored and there was no post mark.

Bill keeps practicing on the mouth organ and at times gets on our nerves, I keep getting fresh jobs on the farm the 2 latest being sheep folding and dung spreading in the hop field. Mum has got a bad finger she scratched it and it has gone septic, she is busy poulticing it. It has been very cold here and frozen over xmas and I'tl turn to snow but thank goodness it didn't?. No doubt by now you are getting into a warmer climate.

Well old sport I must conclude. write as soon and often as you can we all send out love and best wishes for your wellbeing and a happy new year and a safe and speedy return home love mum and dad

PS. Received your xmas card ok cheerio

(Christmas card in photograph section)

Folkestone had taken a hammering from enemy air attacks and cross channel guns with a view to disable the port. Many of the roads around the harbour has sustained substantial damage. The old family home in Dover Street where Aubrey's grandparents lived was completely destroyed. Many of the houses in Warren Road were destroyed over a few days.

When the post war rebuilding took place Warren Road was such a mess it was changed to become Warren Close. Nothing remained of the old buildings and the route of the road was changed to align with the adjacent streets.

The family was safe in the countryside but must have had concerns that their old hometown was taking such a battering, with old friends and family being made homeless. Fred was born in Folkestone and his wife Rose came from Elham just a couple of miles north of the town.

It must have been apparent then that the family would not return to their home town and the realisation of they must adopt the ways of the country people. Farm work was just so different to what they were used to. Sheep folding was something Fred would never have seen before, to those who are not country folk it is the practise of gathering sheep and putting them in temporary penning, so they could control movement on the fields when they were eating turnip tops or similar.

Syd Newing was Rose's brother, they lived at Crocksyard cottages just up the hill from the village of Wingham, he was a farm labourer and in later years a gardener and to be fair, one of the nicest, kindest and gentle people I have ever met. Together with his wife Annie 'Queenie' lived in Wingham for all their married lives, retiring to sheltered housing in the village until their deaths in the 1980s.

I can deduce the Harvey family were friends of the Garretts, the son is mentioned in previous letters from Fred, Harvey junior does not appear in the casualty lists so either he had transferred to another Battery in the Regiment or he managed to escape from Crete unscathed. He would then have been allocated to another unit within the Regiment.

Bill did indeed master the Mouth Organ (Harmonica), for years at Christmas he serenaded the family when I was a child in the 1950s!

Jan 24th '41

No 866845 Gnr AC Garrett R.A.
29894 (C). GHQ 2nd Echelon
C/O Army P.O. 725

Dear Mum and Dad

I hope you received my letter which I sent from our last port of call. Since then we have been sailing in real tropical weather although so far the sun has not been as hot as we expected.

Today for instance it has been quite cold and windy, although we have crossed the line, going through the time honoured ceremony as we did so.

En route we have seen sharks and flying fish around the boat and yesterday we saw probably what was a whale.

I meant to have told you that at our last port of call we were besieged by natives in boats, known as bum-boat wallahs, selling fruit or diving for pennies. A lot of the lads took the opportunity to dispose of their ~~of~~ own or anybody elses spare kit that lay around.

We had the spectacle of bumboats returning empty of fruit but their owners clad in anything from army shirts to coloured Glengarries.

We are stopping at another port shortly so with a little luck this will soon be posted.

We have a daily news sheet here which is compiled from the B.B.C. News Service so we are able to keep up with the war in England. I am glad we are getting an answer to the Night Bomber. The other day we heard there was a blizzard raging in the Straights of Dover. I wonder if its as bad there as it was last winter when we were continually digging out our guns.

I think I told you about all that has happened so far. But expect to hear from me again soon.

I think this is all for now so

Cheerio
Aubrey

(Censor signature unreadable)

All mariners since the 1700s have taken part in the 'Line Crossing Ceremony' where sailors who cross the equator for the first time, take part in a ceremony which includes a series of initiations led by an individual dressed as the mythical character, King Neptune.

The ceremony usually involved random shaving of the head, getting painted and imbibement of the rum ration.

The previous port Aubrey mentions was Freetown, the capital of Sierra Leone on the west coast of Africa. This would have just been a replenishment stop over, probably only for a few hours to take on coal, water and rations.

The local merchants would have taken any opportunity to earn money from passing convoys. During this period the movement of convoys increased tenfold, with reinforcements going to the Far and Middle East, stopping to refuel. The small inland boats would be loaded with local fruit or hand carved goods. They would row out to the ships at their moorings and sell their wares or exchange them for clothing etc.

The winter of 1940 was one of the worst in recorded memory, the snowfall in the south of England was particularly bad. The thought of this was a far distant memory to the soldiers wearing tropical uniforms aboard the convoy.

Feb 11th

No 866845 Gnr AC Garrett R.A.
29894 (C). GHQ 2nd Echelon
C/O Army P.O. 725

Dear Mum and Dad,

At least we are getting near the end of our journey. Almost two months of the seafaring life have made us used to life on board ship but I don't think any of the lads will be sorry to have the feel of dry land under their feet once more.

At our last port of call we were given a spell of shore leave.

I wish you could see some of the sights we saw there. It was a grand place and perhaps in my next letter I shall be allowed to tell you its name and something about the country its ~~next~~ in.

The people we met seem the most hospitable in the world. Several of the Dover lads and I were given a drive into the country by an old Dover College man.

He was very interested to hear about the actions we saw there, and of course we were not behind in telling him of the terrific battles we had to save his old school from the grasp of the Hun. I think he got the impression (after listening to Paddy Iwaid) that the streets of Dover were shoulder high in Jerries Air Force.

Towards the end he began to wonder how Jerry had more planes if we shot down the number that Paddy claimed.

By the way I hope despite Jerries raids the shack is ~~XXX~~ still standing. We hear the raids are not so bad now. But perhaps Jerry is saving them up.

At the moment I have no more to tell you but I will write more as soon as we land.

Hoping you are all in good health and spirits

Cheerio

Aubrey

(Signature of 2Lt Corbett censor)

Looking at the archive[3], the TS now the HMS Canterbury, docked at the South African port of Durban enroot to Port

Tewfik, on the last leg of its journey. Durban had a high number of British expatriates working for the Empire during the 1920s/1940s and this gentleman from Dover College would have been one with a significant job to own a car at that time. It's very interesting that he took the time out to show the lads around the area.

The lads from 223 quite rightly were proud of their exploits at Swingate, perhaps a little over exaggeration aided by some alcohol consumption, accounted for it in this particular case!

Myrtle Cottage
Bramling
Wingham
Nr Canterbury
Feb 3rd 1941

Dear Aubrey,
We were very pleased to receive a letter from you to day dated Dec 27th. We rather expected a letter because I saw Mr Harvey yesterday and he told me he had a letter from his son on Saturday, so Mum was on the lookout for the postman this morning. I was very pleased to get your letter. So you were a bit seasick we expected you would be for you sailed at a bad time of the year but we are glad to hear of your arrival in calmer waters. By our reckoning you should have arrived at your destination. We wonder where you are but no doubt you will be able to let us know in due course. So you were not impressed by the look of the ship you went on but as long as she got you out there she was ok. With regards to your postscript about not telling Bill and Raymond that you were seasick. Raymond won't be able to say much for I must tell you about him. He was put on a barge in the river Humber with a barrage balloon and I suppose it was very rough for he says he couldn't be sick but it affected his head and he says he laid on the floor with water coming through the hatches and the cracks etc falling all over him and he had to go sick and ask to be put on the land and he is now ashore helping to load balloons. We are glad to hear you are well and I'm glad to say we are fairly well but for colds. We have had cloudy skies for a fortnight but yesterday we had a beautiful bright day like spring only to wake up this morning with the wind howling and snow falling again. I didn't go to work until after breakfast and have been dung spreading. We have not had a lot of rain activity a few low raiders sneak over in the clouds during daylight but the nights have been very quiet thank the good lord. But old Jerry lobs some shells well inland. Quite a lot of our planes were up yesterday and over a hundred went on a trip over the channel just to see how Jerry was getting on. There is not a lot of news to tell you we hear from Nannie

every week and she sends her love to you and says she will write to you, they are keeping very well and she asks if she should go back to Folkestone as she is worried about her furniture. I told her to stop where she is while the invasion talk is on. I wonder if it will come and am inclined to think they will have a go and I expect we shall be in a hotspot here but we must stick it out. Bill has been to the pictures this last few Saturdays at Canterbury with his pal Jack. I expect they will go this week as the film the great dictator is on. We haven't heard much about Folkestone lately father said he had heard from his mate Tim who was now drawing the old age pension, but he could not get a job and that it was very quiet there as regards to business. Dennis is still ok we heard last week and he always enquires about you. Does your watch still go alright? and I have had mine done up for myself and one for Bill so we are alright for time now. We hope you had a wireless set aboard so they you could hear the news and get a spot of music.
Grandfather Newing was 74 on Sunday and is still going strong.
Well old son we wish you all the best and will write to you every week and you must write as often as you can and tell us of your doings. We keep getting good news of our lads doings East and are giving old Musso something to get on with. well cheerio from all of us and may God keep us all safe and sound reunite us in peace
Mum, Dad, Bill and Gladys.

This was the first letter to be returned home as 'undelivered deceased' in late July, sending post to the Middle East must have been logistically difficult, many letters must have gone adrift in the chaos of the Crete evacuation. The mailbags would have been received at 89 HAA Regiment HQ for forward transmission to CREFORCE, but for weeks afterwards no one knew who had been killed, missing or prisoner of war and indeed killed in action.

When this letter left home on its long journey, there could have been no hint of the turmoil to come. Fred refers to 'Jerry' as an acquaintance or an old friend, someone they knew or a relative. I would guess that the presence in their lives as a formidable, but yet remote enemy, must have brought a familiarity, albeit at arm's length.

Grandfather attaining the age of 74 seemed to be a milestone, in the 1940s this would have been quite a significant age. The life expectancy during this time would have been mid to late 60[4], for grandfather someone who had worked on the land all his life with the stresses and sheer exhaustion through heavy manual work, was quite an achievement.

Cousin Raymond was selected for aircrew training, he wanted to be a pilot, but in the first couple of weeks he suffered dizziness and after some tests, was found to suffer from what we know today as Labyrinthitis. This brought his desire to fly to an end as he had completed the basic training for servicemen, and as he was out of the normal routine, he was initially posted to the RAF Police but eventually became an operator in a section of balloons. Not the glamorous job he had intended!

The Germans built gun emplacements along the French coast and installed naval guns with similar range capability to our own guns on the cliffs at Dover, the sighting equipment hadn't been modified so although they could hit a town visible 25 miles away, they shots inland were very much hit and miss.

Myrtle Cottage
Bramling
Wingham
Nr Canterbury

Feb 17th 1941
Dear Aubrey

Here we are again and I am pleased say we are all fairly well and we hope you are in the pink. I went to the volunteer Last night and I heard that Mr Harvey had, had a cablegram From his boy saying he had got ten days leave and was in Durban so we guess you are not far from him we hope you stay there for some time and I expect the people there will give you a good time. I have not a lot news for you but one item in the daily express said that nine pubs In Folkestone had been bombed or damaged and 35 had closed due to lack of trade so its hard luck on the beer trade in our old town.

We heard from nanny and Grandfather last Friday they are getting on fare and send their love to you. Grandfather said that after Raymond being bad on a barge and you being sea sick he's afraid his grandsons wont make good sailors. Bill has got to register next Saturday but he has written to the R.A.F to make enquiries about wireless mechanics. Dennis has moved to a fresh billet another farm near his old billet I think the reason he moved was because his people are having two land girls and they want the room for them. Things have been fairly quiet here we still get a lot of warnings during daylight and several bump over at night and we have had a few shells drop well inland but a few miles from us they sound pretty close.

Young Harvey who used to be at Dover with your old crowd is home from Derby on seven days leave.

He said that Maj Butler had left them and he believed he had gone overseas. What do you think about the way our boys are mopping up the wops and only wish we were giving Jerry the same medicine. There is still a lot of invasion talk and I expect they will have a crack at us lets hope he doesn't come our way. Last Saturday night uncle Fred came down and he Bill and I went up to the Eight Bells and played darts Fred beat Bill and then I beat uncle Fred and then uncle Fred and played the landlord and another chap and we won. I was in good form and finished the game by getting seven brake. While we were up the Eight Bells we could see the flashes In the sky? from France where our boys were bombing the channel ports and it went on for hours.

Mum is busy sewing and of course Bill is in his armchair. The 9o/c news is on and the siren has just gone for the nightly blitz. If its quiet I'm going to get a pint I wish you could have one with me. Well cheerio old son all the best love from all of us and may god bless and keep us all safe.

Mum and Dad

PS. Enclosed Dennis' address.

The ten days leave in Durban must have been a welcome change for the lads on board the HMS Canterbury, they had been cramped on board for weeks with no exercise. They had about another week or so on board before they reached their final destination.

The importance of the pubs in Folkestone was not underestimated, for years the army was garrisoned there and soldiers in many of the pubs was commonplace. With the war came restrictions keeping the soldiers in camp or out on long exercises. Of course, the soldiers' units would have been part of the local defence plan, so stationed at key points around the area. Leave would have been minimal.

Another consideration would be that drinking age youngsters would have joined up and could have been anywhere in the world at that time. The was only one brewery in the area in 1940, Mackeson's' was in Hythe, serving the Folkestone and Dover area. I should think they were very close to shutting down[5].

Young Harvey stayed with 223 Battery and following a move shortly after Aubrey left the unit they moved to near Sheffield where the battery split and he went with the section to Derby. I can only surmise that there were two brothers, the elder selected for transfer to 234 Battery whilst the younger remained with 223 Battery. Major Butler was the Officer Commanding the Battery in Folkestone when Aubrey joined up.

When Hitler changed the focus on the attacks on Great Britain, switching to night attacks on cities. Very few flights happened during the day except for reconnaissance and aerial photography flights, but the air raid alarms were set off until the aircraft were positively identified.

The Eight Bells was one of two pubs in the area, the Volunteer a hundred yards down from their house, and the Eight Bells about half a mile away. The Eight Bells served better beer so it was the pub of choice! Uncle Fred lived in Crocksyard next to his brother Syd about a mile away from Bramling.

Myrtle Cottage
Bramling
Wingham
Nr Canterbury
Thursday Feb 27th (1941)

My Dear Aubrey,

I trust this will find you quite well and happy and enjoying the better weather than we have got here we are all fairly well but last week mum and I both had nasty influenza colds and I was at home for 3 days but we are both better and I went to work on Monday but today It has rained hard and I was nearly wet through, by dinner time so I packed up and came home to keep the fire company, Bill registered last Saturday and I think I told you he wrote and volunteered as a wireless mechanic R.A.F. but he has had a reply saying that as he is now registered he will have an interview with an Air Force officer when he is called for a medical exam. We shall be sorry to see him go as it will be so lonely on our own Roll on Peace. We wonder where you are now and what you are up to, look after yourself and lets know if there is anything we can send you. There is not a lot of news to give you, we still get a lot of daylight warnings but we don't see many jerries the sky seems full of our planes but of course at night Jerry comes bumping over as usual and sometimes we have a bolt for our cupboard.

Raymond says they have got a new stunt on and go out on mobile section and there is now a balloon near uncle Sids. We heard from both Nanny and Dennis this week both send their love to you. The meat ration is now only 1/2 per week but we don't do too bad, we manage to get our tummies full of something. Nanny says it is a job to get anything much for poor old Tiny. I always think of him when I get a bone on my plate. Did I tell you in my last letter that Phoebe had bought a budgie for Dennis. We have got him a cage made from a margarine box. it is a pretty blue colour and was lonely at first but mum put a little mirror from a handbag in the cage and it cuts all sorts of capers. It makes company for mum for she keeps talking to it and knows her and whistles to her. But thank goodness it doesn't make so much noise as the one Granny has got. Well we are mopping up old Mussos Empire and we wonder where the blitz Is going to break out next there looks like trouble In the Balkans and our people keep having a go at the invasion ports They were on the job again last night and jerry was bumping about over here I have missed todays post which goes at 5-15.

I see by the Herald that one of your old college chums is in trouble again Wally Cooper. He pinched a bike At Canterbury valued at £7-10-0 and sold it for 30/s to buy presents for his girl. He got six months hard labour and an officer said they didn't want him back in the army So he's found a way to get his ticket, still I reckon he is daft and ought to put in a home instead of prison. Another piece of news is that GHB Diamond Is leaving Folkestone to take up an appointment at Chatham.

I saw Mr Best up here on Sunday he came up to see mother and of course I met him in the pub. He said that the bomb that fell on Burrow Rd damaged a lot of houses in Warren Rd and our windows and doors were shook up a lot. He said a crowd of jerries came over the channel the other week towards Dover and our fighters met them and there was a bit of a scrap over Folkestone but jerry soon cleared off back. There has been a War Weapons week for Canterbury and Bridge-Blean district. Up till last Tuesday the grand total was £312784.2.3 Canterbury itself got £253697-6-6 and our parish of Ickham got £3835 which is wonderful our contribution was two bob so we shall have shares In a spitfire or something. Old Bill came home tonight with his coat wet through he has stood in an old shed nearly all day as it was too wet to work well old son I haven't much to get a letter from you but expect we shall have to wait some time yet, we are in hopes you will stay in Durban for a while, but for all we know you may now be hundreds of miles from there. We send you all the best you wish yourself and the best of luck. love from us all and may God protect and keep us all safe and soon reunite us all. Mum and Dad, best wishes from Bill and Gladys.

Bill finally was accepted as a wireless mechanic, he had a high IQ and was very good at problem solving, so he was a perfect choice.

As the war went on the nightly dash to the Anderson shelter in the garden became a little tiresome, many families took to the cupboard under the stairs when the bombing came a little closer.

One night a low flying bomber flew fairly low over Bramling on its way back to France. This story was recounted to me by a child in the area at that time. It was a dark night with torrential rain so we can only assume it had become lost and was ditching its bombs on the way home.

The bombs were exploding in a string across the fields from the direction of Ickham towards Wingham Well, one did not explode and lies in the front of Bramling House, about three feet from White Cottage and the Newing family, and about three feet from the old entrance.

This was a gravel drive and my source advised me that in the morning, the children were standing round the hole it made trying to see it. This was obviously a defective bomb and due to the height of release and the fact the soil was heavy clay due to the recent rains making the ground soggy, the bomb had gone down several feet and fortunately hadn't exploded.

After a few days the small hole became filled in with gravel due to vehicle movement and the bomb forgotten. For all we know it could still be buried there. This bomb was only 50 feet from the Garrett house, the others in the string fell within 200 yards so the shock waves would have been extensive. They must have had awful memories of their time in Folkestone a few months before.

My source of this information was Fred Bennett my father, he lived next but one to the Garretts in Myrtle Cottages he recounted the story many times over the years but of course we don't know if the bomb disposal teams went to retrieve it after he went to school.

Mobile barrage balloon sites were designed to be a nuisance to the enemy bombers, they could move several times a day and the enemy would see them at dusk on their approach to the target, but they would then move them to try and find the return flight path back to their bases in France.

Uncle Syd's house was at Crocksyard near Wingham on high ground, the small field in front of his house would have been a perfect site for a balloon, I may hasten to add that is not where Raymond was based, he was in the Midlands.

At the time of writing to Aubrey the Italian invasion of Greece had faltered, the Italians were being driven back to Albania. This was not a surprise as the invasion was severely understrength with only eight Divisions being available, the reality was they would have needed at least 20 Divisions to achieve this to have any measure of success.

In addition to being understrength the ports in Albania were not large enough to cope with the sheer volume of sea traffic needed to support such an invasion, primarily only large enough to hold small fishing boats. The invaders hadn't considered the need to improve port facilities after they invaded the country in 1939.

Rationing was becoming more controlled, those living in the country could take advantage of fruit and vegetables in season, but those living in the towns and cities struggled to get the correct balance of fruit and vegetables. Ricketts became a problem having not been seen in the country for many years[6].

Those living in the country usually had larger gardens to grow their own food, as the war progressed the country folk sometimes clubbed together to buy a pig, they fed it from scraps from their mealtimes and when the time came, they shared the rewards, this was sometimes called the 'pig club'.

In the countryside there was more access to eggs, many people kept hens and hen ownership increased to levels never seen before. They were easy to keep, they could be fed on vegetable peelings etc, mixed together with rough bran. This mixture was then boiled and fed to the hens. They also foraged the gardens in their enclosure for the grit they needed to produce strong egg shells.

Catching rabbits and a little 'poaching of pheasants' happened frequently, as evidenced by my great uncle Fred Newing when he was caught and brought before the local Magistrate! It is fair to say those living in the towns found rationing significantly more difficult to cope with than their counterparts in the rural communities.

Rationing of food was introduced in 1939, households had to be registered and ration books were issued. Typically, an adult's ration allowance was one egg, two ounces each of butter and tea, an ounce of cheese, eight ounces of sugar, four ounces of bacon and four ounces of margarine[7]. Not much by today's standards, but families became creative with recipes and the government issued suggestions on innovative ways to make a nutritious meal from next to nothing.

All this was a time consuming activity, you have to remember there were no supermarkets in 1940, all food had to be bought from the butcher, baker, fishmonger, grocer and of course a greengrocer. A trip out to purchase the weeks entitlement could have almost been a day out for many housewives as they were known at that time, especially if they encountered a queue at each shop.

Very few working class people had a car during this time, and even if they had, petrol rationing was introduced in 1939 restricting movement except for essential travel for business deliveries. Doctors and officials engaged in their normal work routines made up a small proportion of the overall population.

The War Weapons Week was a national initiative to get the population to contribute to the ever-increasing cost of war materials. The local council was then known as Bridge - Blean Rural District Council, the event was coordinated through District Councils and put into place by individual Parish Councils.

Bearing in mind it was 1940, raising £3835 from a predominately farming community was indeed quite amazing! There was a scheme whereby the population could purchase a Spitfire Mark 1 for £5000, this was the contract price and the actual costs the Government paid was £8,897.6.6 (pounds shillings and sixpences!) This would be the 2023 equivalent of £250k[8]. Ickham indeed had purchased over half a Spitfire, I am sure they would have been very proud to contribute so much to the war effort.

The total from the whole area is a staggering sum, one pound in 1940 was worth in today's money £53.20 so that figure is mind blowing the national figure raised overall was nearly thirty million pounds, some six hundred million in 2023!

March 6th

Myrtle Cottage
Bramling
Wingham
Nr Canterbury

My Dear Aubrey.

How are you old sport, in the pink we all hope. Glad to say we are all pretty well. As yet we have not heard from you except the letter you sent from mid ocean but there is no time lost yet. I saw Mr Harvey on Sunday and he said they had received another cablegram of saying: Arrived Middle East, alls well, so we are wondering where you have arrived at now. Things look like breaking out a bit now that Jerry has gone into Bulgaria and we hope you don't get into a hot shop. We have had it fairly quiet here. Of course the siren is on and off all day but jerry doesn't get in much in daylight and we have had some good nights although jerry has passed over. Gladys went to Elham with Phoebe on Tuesday to see uncle Ted. He and aunt Daisy are ok and he is a fire watcher. They told Gladys that jerry dropped some of his new flares over our old town the other night and they lit Elham up.

Later,

I left off on Thursday meaning to carry on the next evening but I put it off and hear it is now Saturday. Have been busy in the week digging in the hop fields and it is wet and heavy and the old farmer wants it done piece work and is paying 3/10 per 100 and me not being good at digging I was 8/= short of a weeks work and it took the stuffing out of me even uncle John and some of the old stagers couldn't make a full week and I felt a bit rough so I went and saw the doctor and he put me on the panel and told me to take things a bit quiet, he has put it down on the certificate as neurasthenia but don't worry I am not ill, I think the heavy work is a bit too much for me and if I rest for a week or two I can look around and try and get an easier job. Old Bill is the bread winner now. At the present moment he is busy in the armchair reading a cow poke magazine. I had a pile of books given me today to help pass the time away a lot of them are Picture Post. Yesterday the weather was wet and we were paddling about in mud all day. If you are in Egypt send us a few loads of desert sand to help dry the ground up. Today it is more spring like and we have had a few raids and we heard some AA fire Dover way but jerry doesnt get far inland in daylight and we seem to have hoards of fighters about the sky. We heard from Dennis the other day and he told the people says the people try and make him happy but he gets fed up at times but he then thinks we shall all be together soon and he cheers up again. I expect he gets home sick for he has been away nine months now.

I do wish it was all over but I'm afraid we have got a lot to go through yet. You should see our Sunday joint a piece of beef the size of a saucer and talking of meat, when I was in Wingham this morning I had to laugh to myself at the stock displayed in the window of the butchers which consisted of 2 duck eggs, 1 oxtail and one solitary rabbit, I suppose what meat they had, was cut up and delivered and that was all they had left to sell. We had pork sausages for dinner today, what they do now is to get some breadcrumbs show it to a pig and put them in a skin and call them pork sausages. Bill has at last removed his carcase from the armchair and is now putting some new spokes in his bike wheel. I am enclosing two cuttings from the Herald and a photo of a home guard and some of the gasworks chaps are in it including G. L. B. Diamond. You will note by one of the cuttings that since the Garretts left Folkestone 35 pubs have had to close down. So things are pretty rough in our old town. Poor old nan Grant who live next door to Nannies hadn't had her clothes off for six months and has been put in the infirmary. There is not much news I can give you. Here I am again I lost the post which goes at 4-45 now so I am now finishing off to post now. Our Sunday lay in was ruined today we woke at 7-30 to the noise of planes and then the siren went and we heard AA and machine gun fire so me and mum hopped out of bed but Bill laid tight it didn't last long and I believe it was Ramsgate way and we heard no bombs. We all wish you the best of luck and cheerio old son love from all of us.

Mum and Dad

God protect and give us an early and victorious peace?

Fred refers to being on the panel, before the unemployment benefit colloquially known as 'the dole' getting money was so complicated. Getting a job in the 1940s was quite easy. There was always work if you looked for it and usually locally or a bicycle ride away. If you were unable to work through illness, getting enough money was quite a difficult process.

If you went to the doctor and declared unfit to work through illness or some sort of mental disorder, the doctor applied to a Medical Board and you were summoned to appear before a Board. This consisted of doctors and civil servants who looked at your case and determined whether you should get a state welfare payment. It was not much but it helped a household where others members of the family were working.

The diagnosis of Neurasthenia[9] was not uncommon, I believe it came into being in the 19th century as a safety net for doctors who were faced with many patients who had seem indescribable things in war. In WW1, the number of sufferers rose sharply, their ability to carry on a normal life was minimal or impossible.

Fred of course was one of that number, nowadays his diagnosis would have been Post Traumatic Stress Disorder, but in the 1940s there was no treatment except admission to a Mental Hospital where the treatments were sometimes barbaric to say the least. Fred's brother in law Charlie had a bad case of PTSD and spent most of his life in and out of St Augustine's hospital in Chartham.

I have seen this effect first hand; a friend of mine's father was a medic in the Korean war and suffered badly from the sights he witnessed. When he returned home, he couldn't hold down a job, eventually went on the sick panel where he remained until he was beyond the working age. It had a profound effect on his life.

Fred eventually got a part time job as a funeral home pall bearer, and then part time work as a handyman working for Miles Builders in Wingham until the 1960s when he retired.

For a trained Silversmith/antique shop owner, digging heavy wet clay based soil all day was just not the job for him, he had never experienced manual labour and I suspect John had got him the job as he already worked for the farmer.

Bill reading a 'cow poke' magazine was in fact a Cowboy Comic, readily available back in the 1940s. GLB Diamond was the general manager at Folkestone Gasworks, he is referred to with some reverence so he must have been important to the local area.

Fred's mention of the pubs closing in Folkestone inferred that because the family no longer frequented the establishments, they were somehow responsible for their demise! Not the case of course, the population of Folkestone had decreased with call up and residents moving inland to relatives, and the recent shelling and bombing had taken its toll on these establishments.

Fred and Aubrey had a very similar sense of humour, Fred's description of the pork sausages was typical, the sausages during the war indeed contained very little pork, probably 10% and the remainder was cereal and breadcrumbs. Not particularly nutritious, but in physiological terms a bit fat sausage equalled a fully stomach!

One of the press cuttings still exists and are in the photographs section together with the Gasworks Home Guard.

Date unreadable, postmark March 1941

No 866845 Gnr A Garrett R.A.
234/89 Heavy AA Regt R.A.
Middle East Forces

Dear Mum and Dad.

At least we have reached the end of our long journey and are now under canvas somewhere in the Egyptian desert. After a voyage of nearly nine weeks you can imagine any sort of land, even desert, is a welcome relief to the constant site of the sea. Altogether we had quite an enjoyable voyage but few of us are sorry we left behind the seafaring life.

We are in a huge camp- as far as the horizon there is nothing but tents and sand hills. Units from practically the whole Empire are here with us.

At the moment we are having our first sand storm and the Dhobis or native laundrymen are doing the grand tour of Northern Egypt hunting for our washing. Our tent is also uncertain whether or not to reach the upper stratosphere. We just have to become human tent pegs and hang on. The sand is dying away now but rain has taken its place and its coming down in torrents.

It has never been really hot here yet although we are having a siesta in the afternoon. Actually of course we are having the Egyptian winter and the weather is much the same as July or August in England. In the early morning and at night it Is quite cold; cold enough for us to wear battledress in fact, although the rest of the day we have tropical dress.

There are a couple of immense prison camps near here full of native and Italian troops[10]*. At night they are lit up by thousands of torches, whether or not as an invitation to Wop* *airmen to bomb their own troops I don't know. As yet we have not seen an enemy plane though. Probably there are not enough German airmen in Libya to fly them. There are a lot of troops here resting after a spell at the front. Almost all of them have a poor opinion of the Italians fighting qualities. I hope we shall have a chance before too long to judge for ourselves.*

By the way you will have noticed the change in our address, but I shall get the letters you sent to the old address before long.

I understand it takes about 9 weeks to get a letter home to England by sea, but the Air Mail route should be considerably shorten the time.

I don't think there is any more I can tell you at the moment so,

Cheerio
Aubrey

Signature of A Corbett Lt RA

The HMS Canterbury docked at Port Tewfik on the 16th February 1941. The transit camps in this area covered vast swages of desert[11]. The term desert was not as we think of the Sahara, with shifting dunes and soft sand underfoot. The desert here was flat and hard under the surface although the top was a fine layer of soft sand. Wheeled vehicles would be able to drive on it without sinking.

The word 'Dhobi' is in fact left over from the age of Empire. A Dhobi is a caste group in India meaning washerman. It is derived from the Hindi word Dhoba meaning 'to wash'. The British Army refers to contractors anywhere in the world who do laundry as 'Dhobi wallahs' up to and including my own time in Kosovo in 2002!

The term 'Wop' Aubrey uses to describe the Italian Army soldiers is a slang and derogatory word that has been in circulation for many years.

The word has now disappeared from the English language with the onset of political correctness. When the

Italians changed sides later in the war the term was not used to any extent.

(Received in an official 'Active service' enveloped bearing the stamp of the censor)
March 20th 1941

No 866845 Gnr AC Garrett
234/89th Heavy A.A Regt R.A
Middle East Force.

Dear Mum and Dad,

I have just received two letters from you dated 17th and 21st January.

We had all been looking forward to the first batch of letters from Blighty and at last they have arrived.

Glad to hear you are all doing pretty well at home but I am sorry you were disgraced in a darts match with uncle Harry. When I get back you must take a little of my coaching.

We have been in Egypt now just over a month. They have been giving us 12 hours leave into Ismailia a town on the Suez Canal, but last week they started 3 days leave to Cairo and I am just back with the first bunch. We had a fine time there. The only drawback for white soldiers is that they are besieged by hoards of street Arabs wanting to sell you anything from beads to battleships. Or else blokes come up and ask for "Baksheesh" which means a tip. There are hundreds of little boys in the street who clean your boots for about a half piastre (a piastre is about twopence halfpenny).

One has to be very carefull not to get bad money as every second person in Egypt seems to make his own money. Every shop out here has a marble slab on the counter and when you get any change you bang it on the slab to make sure it is good.

Some perishing swindler gave me a piastre (or Acker as the troops call them) made of lead. So when the next bloke asked me for Baksheesh I gave him my leadacker and he called me Effendi which means sir, little did he know!

We found a good way of keeping the Baksheesh wallahs away from us. Whenever an Arab approached us we used to hold out our hands and shout "Baksheesh" before he could say anything. They would often open their mouths about 3 feet and stand and stare, never heard British soldiers ask for baksheesh before. I guess we foiled them.

We visited a great many places in and about Cairo. Places like King Fiads Palace, The zoo, the Hiegenic Museum, some Mosques (or Mohammedan churches) and of course the Sphinx and Pyramids.

The palace is very much like Buckingham Palace except that standing stiff like ramrods like the guards, the Egyptian sentries lean against lampposts or sit down outside the gates.

In the Mohammed~~da~~ Aly Mosque we were shown cannon balls embedded in the walls that napoleon shot there when he conquered Egypt.

The Sphinx and Pyramids are at a place called Giza about four miles from Cairo. The Pyramids were tombs for the ancient kings of Egypt and the Sphynx, having the head of a man and the body of a lion was worshipped as a God. We took some photos there and if they come out I shall send you them. We climbed the highest pyramid – the Pyramid of Cheops, - in about 20 minutes It is 625 feet high.

Back in camp there is very little work to do. We play a lot of football and cricket and we have just started to play baseball. We are going to have some sports shortly too.

I cant think of anything else to tell you at the moment so

Cheerio

Aubrey

I am sending you a big copy of the phots enclosed.(no longer available)

When Aubrey arrived in Egypt in early February the allied forces were fighting the Italians to the west. The bad news for the allies was that after the Italians were pushed back from Egypt into Libya. Adolf Hitler realised he needed to assist his ally, so the Africa Korps started to arrive in Tripoli on the 11th February 1941. This sudden arrival of the German Army would have serious consequences on the battles to drive the Italians out of Africa.

The Army eventually under its new commander, Bernard Montgomery only managed to conquer the region in late 1943.

Aubrey was in the rear area awaiting deployment to the forward airfields. A period of acclimatisation after a long and tiring sea voyage was the first thing that needed to be done.

A few days leave would have lifted the spirits, climbing the Pyramid in hob nailed boots wasn't exactly ecofriendly, I suspect minor damage to the stone work was done, but they were young and on leave! These days Egypt protects its historic monuments so no further damage can be done.

Cairo now extends right up to the Great Pyramids such has been the growth in population in the years since 1941, his camp would have been close to Ismailia in the desert.

Aubrey's sense of humour is conveyed to his parents in this letter, gaining the upper hand with the beggars would have been a bit of sport to him.

Myrtle Cottage
Bramling
Wingham
Nr Canterbury
March 24th 1941
Monday

Dear Aubrey,

Once again I start my weekly letter but there is not much to report from the Bramling front. A heavy raid on London last Wednesday caused us to sleep downstairs for Jerries were going over every few minutes but nothing happened this way thank goodness. We had a surprise yesterday we hadn't been up long when an important knock came at the front door, and after tidying my hair I opened the door and there stood Doug. He has got seven days leave, he stayed the night. and went back this morning Gladys, Bill and Doug went to the pictures at Canterbury and last night Bill and Doug walked home with Gladys. We were pleased to see him he is now stationed at (id better not say the name) On the letter it is blanked out as an afterthought. *We saw him off this morning by the 9-40 bus and it reminded us of seeing you off. Everyday mum watches for the post more to see if there is a letter from you. We should soon hear now that is if the ship carrying your letter is not at the bottom of the sea. We have lost quite a lot of ships lately we are giving old musso a hiding and it looks like he's losing his empire. We keep wondering just where you are and we expect when you write you won't be able to tell us anything and now nobody can tell what is going to happen in the Balkans but I don't think Hitler will get things all his own way do you? We heard from Dennis last Friday we hadn't heard for nearly a fortnight but he is ok. In his last letter he seemed a bit homesick for he has been away nearly 10 months now. But this time he says don't worry about me mum I can stick it. He said he was going into Newport to have his photo taken. I have got to have another week on the panel but don't feel too bad. I should like to get a different job to farming work. I wrote to the post office but they wrote and said all applications must come through the labour exchange so I shall go and see the manager one day.*

Next day... Tuesday.

Well, I left off yesterday and today I have a bit more news for you. Bill had his papers this morning to go for his medical next Monday at Canterbury. We also had a letter from Nanny and Grandfather they describe an adventure that Raymond had with his barrage balloon during a raid it was hit by shrapnel it fell over the house tops and Ray was climbing over rooftops to free it with the assistance of the fire brigade they got it free and started to pull it in but it caught up again and they lost the balloon and also knocked off chimney pots and damaged rooves and the old women were running after Raymond wanting to know who was going to pay for the damage. Today we went to Canterbury with Gladys it was the first time I have been there since we came here. It was like going into civilisation after being in the wilds. There were lots of people about but most of the big shops close at six. I got some peas and seed potatoes for the garden. It came on to rain while we were there and as we cycled, we got a bit damp coming home.

It is a dark night and still raining and Bill has just gone home with Gladys I expect I shall have to take her home when Bill is called up I hope they don't call him quickly but the 37s have got to register on the 12th of April we got the news today that Jugoslavia has signed some agreement with Hitler so I think things will begin to happen. We hope you won't be in the thick of it you've had your share of the frontline. Well old son I must conclude we all wish you the best of luck and may god keep us all safe love from all of us and lets hope we soon hear from you. Cheerio and thumbs up Mum and Dad.

Doug (Cecil Douglas) Culley was with 4th Buffs and after the evacuation from France his unit was stationed near Sheffield. In late 1940 they moved south and began preparations for the move to Malta later in the year. At some point Doug transferred to the Royal Engineers, but sadly died at sea when the ship he was travelling enroute to Malta was sunk due to enemy action. I have looked at the letter several times and the name of his base is wiped out, but I think it possibly says Gillingham, having held it up to a bright light, this was and still is the home of the Royal Engineers training centre.

Fred writes about 'Musso', this is Benito Mussolini the Italian dictator. Prior to WW2, he wanted to expand his empire to become a 'world leader' but mostly this was delusions of grandeur he saw himself as a latter-day Julius Caesar

Bill receiving his call up papers would have been disheartening for Fred, he was about to lose a second son to the war, Bill's aspiration to become a wireless mechanic came to fruition. Fred refers to 37s, for clarity all those who registered for the call up were given a serial number so they could process people with some sort of order. Bill was a serial 37, so in just over 3 weeks his time had come.

Following basic training he completed his wireless course with very high marks. As a youngster Bill used to build rudimentary crystal radio sets wound to operate on the HF (High Frequency). You could receive the long-distance call from amateur radio enthusiasts hundreds of miles away when using the correct antenna.

Bill also belonged to the Radio Society of Great Britain, the governing and licencing body at that time. I do not have his call sign but his RSGB badge is still in the family.

Following the training Bill only had one posting where he remained for the rest of the war. As a Folkestone lad he would have seen the large white building atop the cliffs at Capel Le Ferne. Unbeknown to him this was a significant building contributing to the war effort. Abbots Cliffe house was in fact a VHF (Very High Frequency) listening station intercepting the shorter-range voice signals in German from across the channel.

Intercepting these signals enabled the authorities to pick up downed aircrew in the channel before the enemy could find them and also, the VHF communications between units gave up important tactical information, passed between unsuspecting commanders. German speakers were recruited to transcribe the messages and pass them to the operations room at Bletchley Park near Milton Keynes, where the code breakers were based.

All this information together provided an insight into enemy movement. Early on in the war this was significant with the avoidance of the U-boat packs hunting the shipping in the vast expanses of the Atlantic.

Bill was posted to Abbotts Cliffe House, part of his duties was to adjust and repair the antennas on the rooftops, several times he was strafed by ME109's trying to repair the antennas. This shook him up and in later years he too suffered signs of undiagnosed PTSD.

The posting was deemed secret, all letters home were given a dummy address somewhere in the north of England. It's ironic that the Garrett family lived in Folkestone for over a hundred years but Bill couldn't tell his mum he was posted so close to home. He had to keep quiet on the few periods of leave he received. Bill didn't have a good war, being shot at whilst hanging off a roof didn't foster a good sense of fair play.

Bill's war medals found their way down the family to me in 2019. The box had been opened but they had never been removed from the packaging, it was clear that he was not proud of his time in service, he was just happy to return home in one piece.

After the war Bill retrained to become a television mechanic, he worked for Rediffusion for many years until his early death in 1972.

Chapter Five – The Battle of Crete

Crete was never in the plan for the troops in North Africa, but with the continuing advance of the German Army down through the Balkans and Greece, it became clear that Crete would likely be a strategic strongpoint. Many of the evacuated troops from Greece went straight to Crete to bolster the small garrison there.

When the tactical situation changed, with the German Army steadily moving down through Greece, it was decided to strengthen the defences and move sufficient men and equipment the hundred miles or so from Alexandria, summoning that many ships at short notice would have been a huge logistical challenge.

The Germans also would have realised that a build up of forces could ultimately give the allies a head start to the distance to their oil fields in Romania, currently long range targets from North Africa barely within range.

Postmarked 9 May 1941

No 866845 Gnr AC Garrett
234/89th Heavy A.A Regt R.A
C/O. Army Post Office 299
Middle East Forces.
May 1st 1941

Dear Mum and Dad,

Since I last wrote to you we have been transported from the desert to a lovely island in the Mediterranean. You can imagine that after our spell of sand and heat and smells we are all heartily glad to see green grass and trees and more. Our gun site is about the most lovely I have seen. We are ringed around with 8000ft. mountains which even now in May have snow on their peaks.

The inhabitants are a set of bloodthirsty looking people almost all of whom wear breeches with baggy seats and jack-boots.

The country is a land of oranges and eggs and a wine that tastes like sour port. Unfortunately there is no beer!

Almost all the people are small farmers and their fields have stone walls around them instead of hedges.

We have been in action a few times but it is so quiet after Dover that we hardly know there is a war on. There are several air raid alarms but we rarely see any planes. I hope air raid activity over England has slackened and the old shack is still standing.

I suppose that my letters are slow to arrive. I have had three from you so far- the last dated 24th of January. I hope all is well at Grannies, you might send them my love. I hope it wont be long before I hop on the bus and see the old lane again. I bet it looks lovely now. Is the beer still as vile at the old "Volunteer" "I wonder"? They had better change it when I get back as you remember I never liked it. By the way you might polish up the darts playing for when I stage a comeback.

We have a couple of puppies near the gun site that we look after. One of them is very much like old Tiny when he was younger. You must let me know how he is getting on in his country estate. I expect he doesn't know me ~~k~~now. He probably dug himself a shelter for himself in readiness for Air Raids if he is as windy as our pups. Every time we have a shoot "Gunner and Shrapnel" as we call them pass nearby they very nearly pass bricks. We are thinking of posting someone to look after them every time Jerry come over.

You will notice that our address keeps changing. It has changed again so I will write it again at the end. I really cant think of anything more to write now. By the way I believe they are speeding up the letters too and from the Middle East so perhaps you will hear from me a little more often.

But for now.

Cheerio

Aubrey

The new address is.

No. Name.

234 Hvy. A.A. Bty.

Middle East Forces Z.

Aubrey describes the Cretan national dress to a tee; it was worn as everyday clothing until well into the early 1960s when more practical fashion arrived.

When it became clear that the island of Crete would be of strategical interest to the Axis Forces, plans were made to garrison the island to prevent occupation. The Ploesti Oil Fields in Romania were essential to the German forces, this was well within bomber reach from the airfields on Crete so removing the threat was of paramount importance to them.

The Axis Forces were moving south from the Balkans through Greece and clearly it would only be a matter of time before Crete was under occupation. The advantage the allied forces had at that time was the ability to decode the 'top secret' Morse Code messages the German High Command used to send orders and logistical movements.

This information was only available to the high level commanders and when the invasion plans of Crete were being formulated, gave the allied forces time to plan a defence strategy.

General Sir Bernard Freyberg was tasked to lead this defence force known as CREFORCE or Force Z. The necessary elements were detached from the existing units in the Middle East and all available transport ships were assembled in Alexandra for the short journey to Crete.

234 Battery received orders to move to Amiriya, a few miles southwest of the port of Alexandria. Amiriya at this time was a staging area, an RAF camp and later became a casualty clearing station.

They set out on the 15th April and arrived two days later on the 17th April late in the afternoon after a dusty and long journey from their holding area. It seems that 234 were randomly selected for detachment as by now all three batteries were fully up to strength[1].

On the 23rd of April, 234 Battery were allocated transport ship '400', the old Irish sea ferry the Ulster Prince, requisitioned by the Royal Navy in 1940. This ship had been an Irish sea ferry, operating the route between Liverpool and Belfast from 1936 after she first came into service. Sadly, she ran aground later in the year only to be bombed and destroyed.

After waiting for all the force transports to be loaded, proceeded to Crete under a destroyer escort. The twelve officers and 347 RA personnel had to sit on open well deck with zero shade. The Australian infantry with them were fortunate to be able to be partly shaded at the rear of the ferry.

The troops only had with them their personnel equipment and a huge cargo of rations. The heavy equipment, guns, vehicles and ammunition were on different vessels so there was nothing to do but wait for it all to catch up When they arrived in Suda Bay on the 24th they began the unloading process, they had docked next to an oil tanker and the crew became anxious when JU87 Stukas began attacking. The ship was cleared urgently but only half of the rations could be unloaded before the ship set sail to escape attack. From there 234 Battery marched about a kilometre south to an olive grove (just behind where the CWGC is today) that still remains today.

The area was known as 42nd Street near the village of Tsikalaria, named in true soldier style from the name of the 42nd Squadron, Royal Engineers unit that was based there in 1940. There was a stage show of the same name on Broadway at that time so the real origins are now lost in the mists of time.

151 Battery were already established, having arrived a few days earlier. They took some of the troops from 234 to their gun positions to assist them until their own guns arrived and were fully functional. The guns at this stage were in transit together with their transport, rations and ammunition. Bully beef and hardtack biscuits[2] were the order of the day! After a few days the food ration began to dry up, the Germans were so effective at hitting the ships in Suda Bay, the rations ended up either blown to smithereens or on the bottom of the bay.

Water was also in short supply, suddenly the island had to provide for 40,000 extra troops in short order, many arrived from Greece a few weeks before Aubrey landed at Suda Bay. It was rationed to two pints per man per day, one was for the ubiquitous tea brew and the other used for drinking and washing.

Twenty four hours later, they were in a transit camp, located within the 5 (New Zealand) Brigade area, later in the day they were machine gunned by two ME109's but fortunately didn't sustain any casualties. Left Troop moved on foot up to the proposed gun site and began digging defensive trenches, this was a journey of several kilometres steadily going up into the mountains, not an easy task.

It was incredibly hard work in the heat with rocky and heavy soil, together with limited access to water, made it an impossible task. Right troop went slightly North to a position on the flank of 5 Brigades position two days later, the guns arrived (26th April) and by the end of the day were in position on both sites ready for action. Within minutes the guns were firing against Stukas.

You can sense the excitement for his first visit to Crete, for a lad coming from a seaside town in Kent, a Greek island would have appeared to be paradise. The White Mountains are a magnificent sight with the snow still adorning the peaks even in the early summer.

The wine he refers to may be Retsina, widely available all over Greece. It has an underlying flavour of pine needles, most definitely an acquired taste. It could possibly be the spirit Raki, very potent so the habit of sinking it like pints of beer would have given him a headache of massive proportions!

It is interesting to note the calm manner which Aubrey portrays in his letter, the area around the gun sites would have some serious fortifications dug where they could, but most of the defences around Left top position was just rocks and boulders stacked up. A trench network was dug on a very rocky ground. The War Diaries indicate much more action seen than his letters suggest. I suspect he was trying to alleviate the worry for his parents.

The first chance for Aubrey to write home was a week after their arrival, such was the intensity of the preparations. The physical movement of ammunition with work parties would have been one of the primary tasks, bearing in mind the gun site was on the top of a mountain with only a track to access it. The weather was also quite hot but nowhere near as intense as the desert they had just left!

The beer at the Volunteer in Bramling was notoriously dubious, the stories locally always reflect this, Dicky Mayes the landlord didn't bother cleaning his pipes. The constant stream of farm labourers clearly didn't have discerning palates, just thirsty after a hard day's labour in the fields!

Stray dogs are still a problem in Crete, many British ex pats look after them now and send them back to the UK to rehome them. Quite an industry these days. There is a photograph in the IWM (Imperial War Museum) archive of Gunner and Shrapnel with two unidentified gunners.

Aerogram (arrived 20th July)

234 Hvy Bty
MiddleEast
Forces Z

May 19th 1941

Dear Mum and Dad,

Having a glorious time. Wish all of you were with us. Hope you are all in good health and spirits. Trust that old Jerry is still giving a wide berth to the old homestead. Have moved from the land of the flaming desert but can't say where.

Unlike England we have great difficulty and finding anything to shoot at. Please note change of address. Hope old Bill is still Master Navigator of the inland Waterways. By the time I get back he should be First Sea Lord or at least Second Sea lord. Remember me to all at Grannies. We all wish we could see Blighty again, but I suspect it will be a long time yet. So good bye now.

Cheerio

Aubrey

Signature of censor
HP Stebbings

This was Aubrey's final letter home. It is interesting it was written the day before the battle started in earnest. The War Diary states the guns were in action all day firing at bombers that were attacking the airfield at Maleme and the capital ships at anchor in the bay to the east. You can only imagine the stress they were all under at this point, they all knew the invasion was coming, they had been moving ammunition from the supply wagons and firing the guns frequently.

As Aubrey was a GPOA (Gun Position Officers assistant), he would have been taking messages on foot to the guns, answering the telephone and I assume the radio, extremely busy period he must have been exhausted. The letter he sent previously on the 1st May mentioned he had moved to Crete and all but name, it is hard to imagine the effect of the forthcoming invasion was having on the men. Clearly, Aubrey had forgotten he had explained this in the letter eighteen days earlier.

By now the defenders would have an insight and expected date of the assault and nerves would have been at breaking point. The weather was fine and the temperature average 32^{0}celsius which would have taken a toll both on morale and the sheer physical exhaustion of working at full pace for hours on end.

During the few rest breaks everyone was advised to write a letter home knowing it would be many days before mail could be taken from the island and posted on. By know some commanders had the information that Bernard Freyberg received some four weeks earlier, i.e., the actual date of invasion.

It is ironic that the officer who censored this letter was killed on the 24th May, four days after Aubrey.

On the evening of the 19th the German bombers became more frequent and the Battery was in action all night. One gun was used so much the barrel burst[3].

The existence of the two heavy anti-aircraft gun sites would not have gone unnoticed by the Germans through the extensive aerial photography undertaken over the preceding days. Knocking out these gun sites was imperative to ensure the free passage through to the main objective, Maleme airfield.

There were forays into the area before dawn by both DO 17s and Stuka bombers to draw the fire from the gunners. Although the Sperry predictors and the Vickers range finders did a good job it was difficult to traverse the guns quickly to engage the lower targets without resetting the whole system. This proved to be critical because at first light, the JU52's flew down the bay to drop the initial wave of parachutists on to Maleme airfield.

All the gun crews could do was watch this initial wave as they flew so low, they couldn't depress the guns low enough to engage them. Left troop were on the hills at over 600 feet from sea level, slightly higher than the aircraft were flying. The barrels could not depress that low and even if they could they would have fired directly on to the Right troop to the rear of the port across the bay where Right troop were based.

Within an hour the glider forces arrived directly onto Right troops position, the area was flat and had very few trees in 1941, ideal for a landing zone, a significant battle ensued and some hand-to-hand fighting. Bearing in mind the defenders only had two Lewis guns and one rifle per eight soldiers to defend themselves with. Most of the troops took cover in the trenches unable to defend themselves.

One of the gliders landed on the position very heavily and the wings broke off, as it careered across the gun position the Lewis gunner, Gunner Bob Reed raked it with gunfire. When it came to rest all the occupants were either killed or seriously wounded[4].

The glider force was able to bring some support weapons and they initially attacked the gun sites with 81.4 mm mortars. After the final barrage Aubrey stood up to see what was happening as the final round landed inches from him and he met his demise[5].

The troop officer, lieutenant Stebbings who censored the last aerogram Aubrey sent, was killed with the whole gun crew. Up to this point he had been picking off German troops with one of the few rifles to great effect. It is not known when his uncle Colonel Stebbings, Commanding Officer of the Regiment was made aware of his demise, but he visited gunner Charles Milner in hospital a few days after he arrived back in Egypt and asked about the events of that day[6].

The position was assaulted and over thirty unarmed allied troops were killed huddled in their trenches on Aubrey's gun troop, probably in retaliation for the death of the crew and occupants of the glider. The command post roof was blown off by a mortar and shortly afterwards they were surrounded. A German officer who could speak good English shouted to them to come out and they would be spared.

The remaining personnel came out and once in the open, one of the Germans opened fire, an officer, Lt Coccolis and some gunners were killed and three were wounded, the German who fired his schmeisser shot one of his own troops so his colleagues stopped him firing further, and the remaining defenders were rounded up[7]. Later in the day the position was re taken by Royal Marines.

Those 234 men now prisoners could only watch, disarmed and centralised were shocked to see the marines, even more shocked when they realised that the marines were from Deal Barracks, some half a mile from the 234-detachment drill hall. Many knew each other from their mutual trip to the pubs in Deal

Some soldiers and officers managed to withdraw but the majority where either captured or killed. Two of the troop officers and a small group of soldiers from Left troop managed to escape across the mountains to the south side of the island, picked up and returned to Egypt. After a period of rest and re-equipping they were sent to join other anti-aircraft Royal Artillery units as battle casualty replacements. The survivors of Right troop marched to Sfakia in pairs or small groups of three, many were late for the final Naval vessel and were captured. It must have been humiliating to have to retrace their route as POWs.

Lieutenants Sutton and Corbett managed to complete resumes of their time in Crete, which fortunately survive as an annex to the War Diary, I have added these to the annexes so readers can get a better picture of that fateful day. They provide an interesting perspective of the events leading up to the battle and the subsequent operation to defend the island.

Lt Corbett mentions he had been wounded, but in reality, he suffered a major wound as he was shot through the mouth and lost many teeth. He was in hospital for some months, and was awarded a MC for his actions on that day.

The German troops who took the positions were Wehrmacht regular forces who judging by their weapon scales were trained as commandos or similar. Each soldier carried a luger pistol and a schmeisser 9mm sub machine gun, this indicates they were specialist troops.

Undoubtably the casualties would have been much less if the unit scales of weapons had been better but this was based on the fact that anti-aircraft guns were deemed to be 'rear troops' far behind the forward battle area and the need for close protection was unnecessary.

Additional Bren guns were issued on the arrival in Egypt mainly for air defence but that wasn't enough. If each soldier was armed and platoons of infantry was attached to the gunners the outcome that day would have been so very different. Indeed, the course of the battle may have been different because if the guns had remained in action the JU52 carrying the paratroopers would have taken significant casualties.

The lessons learned in Crete were acted on and in future actions the guns were protected from ground assault so the guns could keep firing.

After the battle and the dust settled, it is quite moving to understand what happened to 234 Battery, of the 359 that landed in troop ship 400, the majority didn't make it back to

Alexandria. Seventy officers and men of the unit were killed, many more were taken prisoner or still classified as missing.

The majority were wounded with the remainder making the long overland journey through the mountains to Sfakia to be lifted off the island by the Royal Navy. This operation was complete on 1st of June because enemy activity was unsustainable around the bay.

82 Years later

The author visited Crete in March 2023 to look at the areas where both gun troops were located.

The Left troop position is high on a cliff some 600 feet above sea level. The four gun positions were located around the ruins of an old fort. This fort has subsequently been refurbished and is now a municipal building used for weddings etc.

The four areas of hard standing for the guns have now been paved over as tourist viewpoints. The stones and large rocks are still nearby where the defensive walls once stood. This position had a fantastic view to the east but it was very exposed, it must have been difficult to see the bombers dropping from the sky with the sun behind them. The view of Suda Bay and down the coast is spectacular and all these years later hard to imagine the conflict and struggles that went on here.

After a few days the troop moved approximately 700 yards to the west to slightly more protected position. Having been up to the fort it is hard to see how they communicated with Right troop, behind the post and Battery HQ in Chania. There was field telephone connected by line between Right troop and Battery Headquarters, but the distance to the fort was too great.

Looking in the records it is not clear how they did this but a supposition by the author is they used a wireless set no 18. This was a manpack High Frequency radio designed for long distance use, highly effective in the withdrawal of Dunkirk a year earlier.

Over the years the roads and tracks have changed making it difficult to pinpoint the Right troop positions but after some careful map overlaying, we found it during our tour.

Looking at the ground, it is in an unusually flat area, ideal for the DS230 gliders the enemy force used to dominate the area. The area is approximately 250 metres to the monastery where initially the wounded were taken for help. When Right troop were dug in the area was just fields with a few olive trees around, today it is an established productive olive grove sectioned by wire fences.

Fortunately, the car repair garage adjacent to the grove appeared to own the ground around so we obtained permission to walk through the trees to the back of the site where the command post would have been located. After the battle the Germans would have bulldozed the defensive positions and filled in the trenches.

A temporary grave site was established utilising the trenches. Some bodies were never found after they were moved later in the war, the feeling locally is some of the soldiers are still laying in what was a defensive trench to this day. There is a sense of peace and serenity there, the noises of the road and industry a few hundred yards away seem silent in the olive grove.

This olive grove was the place where Aubrey and many of his colleagues fell, he could still be there for all I know, a very peaceful place on an island so far away from his home town of Folkestone.

Chapter Six - The search for Aubrey

After the aerogram dated 19 May the family were concerned that they had not heard from Aubrey, they were well aware the war was progressing and reports of the various battles were reported in the national papers. For Fred, being on 'the panel' meant he had quite a bit of time on his hands so he would have scrutinised every snippet of information to try and work out where Aubrey was based[1].

Details of the successes and failures in North Africa were on the front page of the papers daily, Crete did start to feature but it was not until the battle finished did it get any real coverage. Fred must have made the assumption that Aubrey was on an island so he would have assumed that it was Crete. The daily papers would have been scrutinised and assumptions made.

As well as letters the family sent postcards to Aubrey, they were saying much the same as the letters but written by Rose, this one below is a snapshot of those sent back after many months. Letters were sent via ships going round the Horn of Africa, but post cards were sent via Air Mail, thus arriving in less than a week.

Myrtle Cottage 18/6/41

Dear Aubrey,

*Hope this will find you still OK, we are all well. Have still not heard from you since your letter dated March 20th. Doug Culley was home on leave and came to see us on Sunday and stayed the night. Hope you have received some of our letters & one from Dennis. Weather has been lovely and Bill looks like a Nig*er. Not much news for you, everything is much as usual. We all hope you are well and happy & and shall be glad to receive your next letters. No doubt some have been lost.*
Keep smiling old son. Love from Mum and Dad.

This post card indicates none of Aubrey's letters from Crete arrived promptly, this card was returned with all the others sometime in August. The letters from Crete likely arrived after they were notified of his death which would have been a cruel blow to the family.

A large proportion of letters and postcards arrived back at the family home undelivered, with the fluid situation in Crete the parent unit (89 HAA Regiment) in Egypt would have delayed sending the mail forward to Crete, this postcard below shows just how unceremoniously the return journey would have appeared to the family. They were all stamped like this!

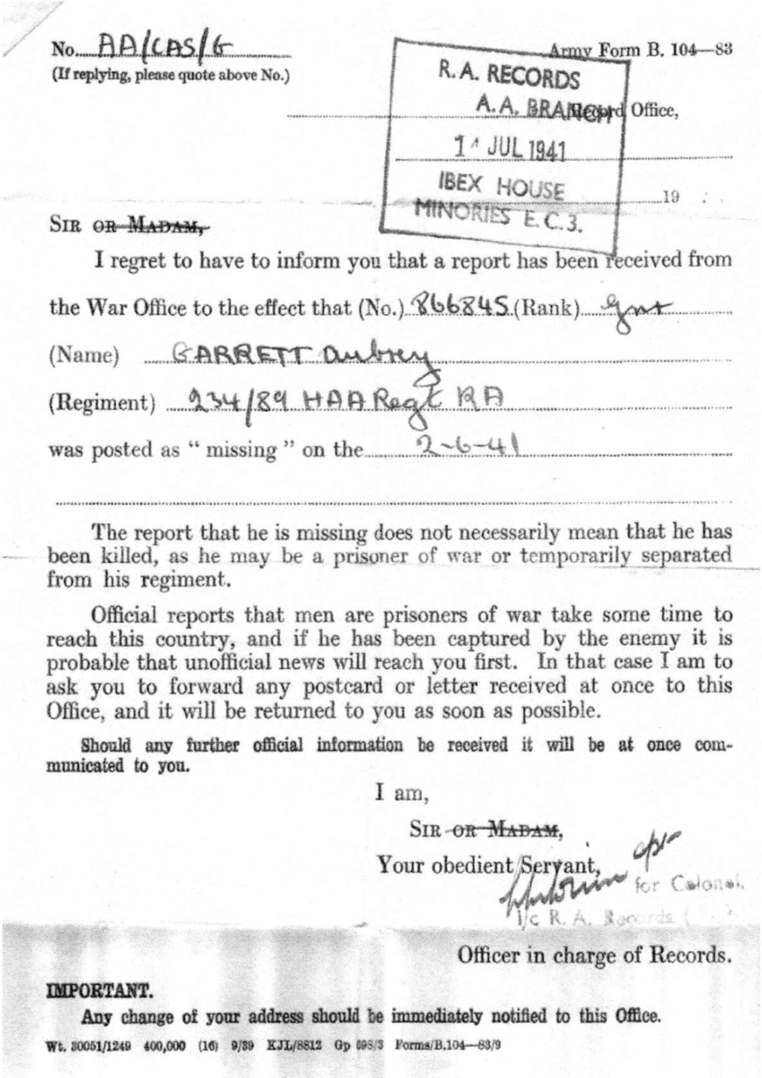
No. AA/CAS/6 Army Form B. 104—83

(If replying, please quote above No.)

R.A. RECORDS
A.A. BRANCH
Record Office,
14 JUL 1941
IBEX HOUSE
MINORIES E.C.3.
19

Sir ~~or Madam,~~

I regret to have to inform you that a report has been received from the War Office to the effect that (No.) 866845 (Rank) Gnr

(Name) GARRETT Aubrey

(Regiment) 234/89 HAA Regt RA

was posted as " missing " on the 2-6-41

The report that he is missing does not necessarily mean that he has been killed, as he may be a prisoner of war or temporarily separated from his regiment.

Official reports that men are prisoners of war take some time to reach this country, and if he has been captured by the enemy it is probable that unofficial news will reach you first. In that case I am to ask you to forward any postcard or letter received at once to this Office, and it will be returned to you as soon as possible.

Should any further official information be received it will be at once communicated to you.

I am,

Sir ~~or Madam,~~

Your obedient Servant,

[signature] Capt for Colonel, i/c R.A. Records

Officer in charge of Records.

IMPORTANT.

Any change of your address should be immediately notified to this Office.

Wt. 30051/1249 400,000 (16) 9/39 KJL/8812 Gp 698/3 Forms/B.104—83/9

They wrote letters to him as usual and looked out for the postman every day. On the 15th of July, a letter arrived from Royal Artillery records stating that Aubrey was missing in action on the 2nd of June, six weeks earlier. The letter explains that he may not be dead but a prisoner of war or just separated from his unit.

The discrepancy with the dates coincided with the declaration of the end of the operation, and the confusion around the evacuation realised many flaws in the army system, completely beyond anyone's control.

The returning soldiers and officers from the unit would have been dispersed around various hospitals and transit accommodation, it would have been many days before the Operations Officers from 89 Regiment would have found them and interviewed them.

Questions such as 'who did you see get killed?' where were you when this happened etc. First hand experiences would have been cross checked with others experiences before any formal word would have been back through the system. Initially a cross refence to who had returned from Crete and those not in Egypt would have generated the 'missing' letter.

Fred and Rose would have hoped that Aubrey would have been captured so they checked the post every few days for letters but sadly nothing was delivered. It would be many days before the confirmed as killed telegram arrived.

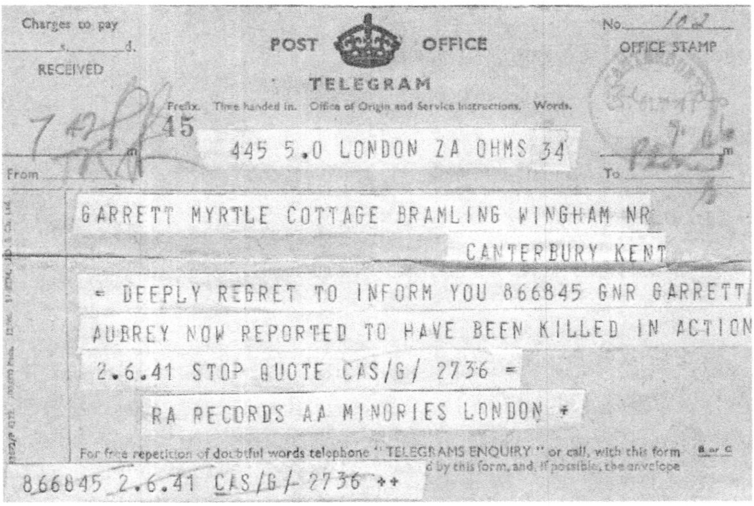

Charges to pay
s. d.
RECEIVED

POST OFFICE
TELEGRAM

No. 142
OFFICE STAMP

Prefix. Time handed in. Office of Origin and Service Instructions. Words.

445 5.0 LONDON ZA OHMS 34

From
To

GARRETT MYRTLE COTTAGE BRAMLING WINGHAM NR
CANTERBURY KENT

= DEEPLY REGRET TO INFORM YOU 866845 GNR GARRETT
AUBREY NOW REPORTED TO HAVE BEEN KILLED IN ACTION
2.6.41 STOP QUOTE CAS/G/ 2736 =
RA RECORDS AA MINORIES LONDON +

For free repetition of doubtful words telephone "TELEGRAMS ENQUIRY" or call, with this form ... by this form, and, if possible, the envelope

866845 2.6.41 CAS/G/- 2736 ++

Fred knew in his heart that this was the start of a long process of writing letters, and had a profound effect on his health. On the 23rd of July a telegram arrived at the family home during the early evening, delivered by the local village policeman. This was the confirmation that Aubrey had been killed on the 2nd of June.

The family were in a state of shock, Fred's PTSD kicked in and he was inconsolable. The telegram still showed the date as the 2nd June, the evacuation was completed by the 1st June, so it can be assumed as dates were fluid this was used as a base line until all the facts had been established. Aubrey was in fact killed early on the morning of 20th May as the invasion was beginning.

Fred would have immediately written to the Royal Artillery records office asking where his son was buried, this became an obsession of his for many years, he just needed to know his son had a grave.

The sight of bodies being blown to pieces in the trenches of WW1 held a lasting vision to Fred, he hoped his son hadn't been killed in such a horrific way.

All around the area many families were receiving the same news, several soldiers came from Folkestone one would have assumed that many of them would have met up in each other's houses, poring over the telegrams trying to get sense from a surreal situation.

All this added to the 'fog of war' on the home front, it would be well after the end of the war that the truth and the missing pieces of the puzzle, would be known.

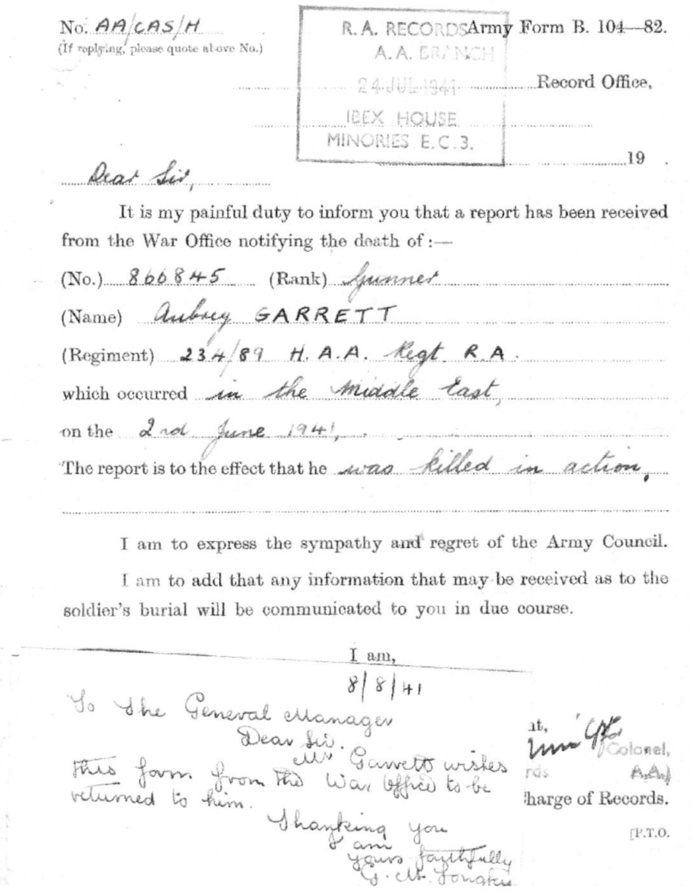

No. AA/CAS/H
(If replying, please quote above No.)

R. A. RECORDS A. A. BRANCH 24 JUL 1941 IBEX HOUSE MINORIES E.C.3.

Army Form B. 104—82.

Record Office,

19

Dear Sir,

It is my painful duty to inform you that a report has been received from the War Office notifying the death of :—

(No.) 866845 (Rank) Gunner

(Name) Aubrey GARRETT

(Regiment) 234/89 H. A. A. Regt R. A.

which occurred in the Middle East,

on the 2nd June 1941,

The report is to the effect that he was killed in action,

I am to express the sympathy and regret of the Army Council.

I am to add that any information that may be received as to the soldier's burial will be communicated to you in due course.

I am,

8/8/41

To The General Manager
Dear Sir,
Mr Garrett wishes this form from the War Office to be returned to him.
Thanking you
I am
Yours faithfully
G. M. Fonatus

...nt,
Colonel,
...rds (A.A.)
...harge of Records.

[P.T.O.

This is the official letter sent as a follow up to the telegram, at this stage the War Office are still showing the assumed date of death as 2nd June 1941.

Ref:- NE/DE/1741

OFFICE FORM No.192A.

Regimental Pay Office,
Great Central Street,
LEICESTER.
4/8/1941.

Dear Sir/Madam,

In consequence of the death of :-

No. 866845 Rank GNR Name GARRETT. A. Unit 234/89 HY. AA.

already notified to you, of which I have learned with much regret, you will doubtless wish to know, without delay, your position in the matter of the allowances payable to you.

The Voluntary Allotment at present being paid to you on his behalf will be continued until 26.10.41 as 1/- per week.

Will you therefore kindly return your Allowance Order Book in the envelope enclosed herewith, after you have received the payment dated 20-10-41

Yours faithfully,

[signature] J.
for Regimental Paymaster
(CRA. & A.A. Branch) R.A.

To:- Mrs. R Garrett
Myrtle Cottage
Brambley Wingham Nr Canterbury.

Aubrey would have made a monthly allotment of one shilling a week for his parents which was worth in today's world, about two pounds. They could draw this at Wingham Post Office, there was no electronic transferring of money in those days, just an allowance book with tear off perforated slips to account for the money issued. A warrant or a postal order was the only other means of awarding money from official sources.

The system has a strange way of addressing the financial things before the human side, Fred would have wanted to know more details about Aubrey's death and most certainly have written to the War Office immediately after the official notification was received, the receipt of this would not have been received well[2]. Yes, they were owed money but Fred would have felt annoyed that all they seemed to care about was finances.

The reality was the paymaster in Battery headquarters would have most likely lost or destroyed the pay records, so assumptions were made after the troops were back in Alexandria. In some accounts soldiers in hospital were paid three times their salary while others didn't receive anything. One must assume that this eventually resolved itself once the control of the pay went back to 89 HAA Regiment.

Soldiers were issued pay which would be kept safe, but the chaos of the withdrawal many of these would have lost. Some soldiers arrived back in Alexandria in not much more than their underclothes, pay was the least of their worries.

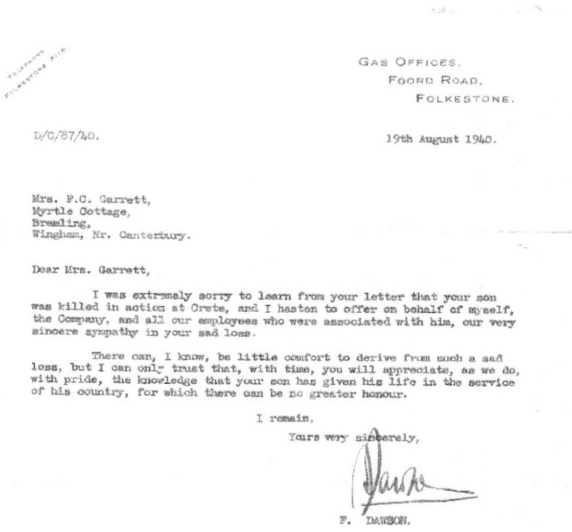
Telephone Folkestone 3110.

Gas Offices,
Foord Road,
Folkestone.

D/C/87/40.

19th August 1940.

Mrs. F.C. Garrett,
Myrtle Cottage,
Bramling,
Wingham, Nr. Canterbury.

Dear Mrs. Garrett,

I was extremely sorry to learn from your letter that your son was killed in action at Crete, and I hasten to offer on behalf of myself, the Company, and all our employees who were associated with him, our very sincere sympathy in your sad loss.

There can, I know, be little comfort to derive from such a sad loss, but I can only trust that, with time, you will appreciate, as we do, with pride, the knowledge that your son has given his life in the service of his country, for which there can be no greater honour.

I remain,

Yours very sincerely,

F. DAWSON.

The Gasworks in Folkestone where Aubrey was working prior to call up had been informed that several of their employees would not be returning[3], the manager sent this letter to the family. The last paragraph would have been no comfort to a grieving family, I am sure.

Tel. No.—Liverpool Wavertree 4000.

Any further communication on this subject should be addressed to :—
The Under-Secretary of State,
The War Office
Casualty Branch,
Blue Coat School,
Church Road,
Wavertree,
Liverpool 15
and the following number quoted.

OR/39440/D. R. (Casualties)

THE WAR OFFICE
CASUALTY BRANCH,
BLUE COAT SCHOOL,
CHURCH ROAD,
WAVERTREE,
LIVERPOOL 15.

25th August, 1941.

Sir,

With reference to your letter dated 29th July, 1941, addressed to the Officer-in-Charge, Royal Artillery Records, I am directed to inform you, with regret, that no further information has been received regarding the death of No.866845, Gunner A.Garrett, Royal Artillery, other than that he was Killed in Action on 2nd June, 1941, while serving in Crete.

I am to convey to you an expression of sincere sympathy in your great loss.

A separate communication will be addressed to you regarding the death certificate.

I am,
Sir,
Your obedient Servant,

Mr. Garrett,
Myrtle Cottage,
Bramling,
Wingham,
Near Canterbury.

The chaos of the withdrawal and the fluidity of the system was unavoidable, yes, the Army knew he was dead but so were thousands of others worldwide, it was a major administrative nightmare trying to pin down the reality of what mattered to the families, i.e., where and when was their loved ones had been killed.

They would never know how he died; it was many years after their death did the full picture come to light. In today's world it would have been much simpler as we have technology to get information from all around the world, in 1941 the only form of communication was by letter and telegram.

Tel. No.: Wavertree 4000.

Any further communication on this subject should be addressed to:—
The Under-Secretary of State,
The War Office (Effects Branch)
Blue Coat School,
Wavertree, Liverpool, 15,
and the following number quoted.
D/49072 (Effects)

THE WAR OFFICE,
BLUE COAT SCHOOL,
WAVERTREE,
LIVERPOOL, 15.

27th August, 1941.

Sir,

In reply to your letter of the 29th ultimo addressed to the Officer i/c Records, I am directed to inform you that as soon as written confirmation of the death of the late No. 866845, Gunner A. Garrett, Royal Artillery, is received from the Middle East a Notification of Death will be sent to you.

Any enquiry regarding pension should be addressed to the Secretary, Ministry of Pensions, Norcross, Blackpool.

Your enquiry regarding the place and circumstances of your son's death has been passed to the Department concerned and a separate communication on this subject will be forwarded to you in due course.

I am,
Sir,
Your obedient Servant,

[signature]

Mr. F. Garrett,
Myrtle Cottage,
Bramling,
Wingham,
Near Canterbury,
Kent.

Such was the intensity of Fred's letter writing the War Office sent similar letters within a couple of days, Fred was frantic his state of mind was fragile and he became quiet and withdrawn. Aubrey had a small life insurance policy with the Tunbridge Wells Mutual building society which he paid into weekly, I suspect the mutual society had asked the family for a death certificate so they could tie up loose ends and make a payment.

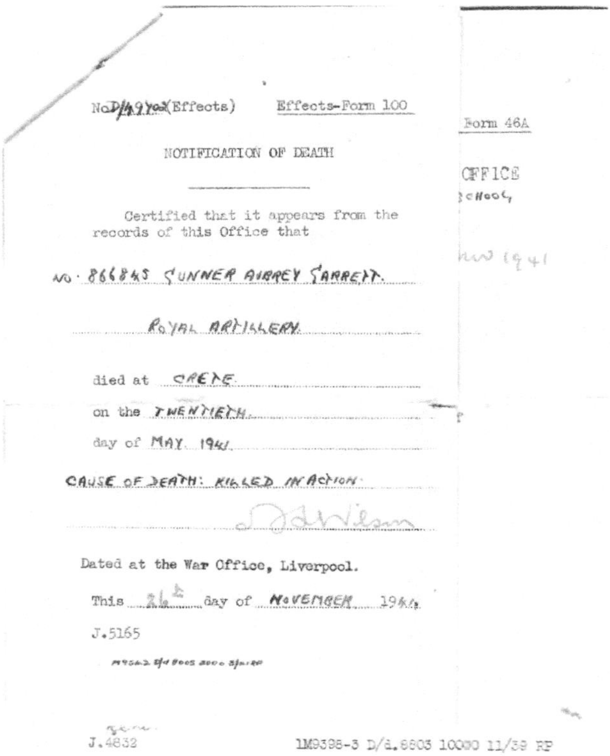
No.D/49Y02(Effects) Effects-Form 100

Form 46A

NOTIFICATION OF DEATH

OFFICE

Certified that it appears from the records of this Office that

No. 866845 GUNNER AUBREY GARRETT.

ROYAL ARTILLERY.

died at CRETE.

on the TWENTIETH.

day of MAY 1941.

CAUSE OF DEATH: KILLED IN ACTION.

Dated at the War Office, Liverpool.

This 26th day of NOVEMBER 1941.

J.5165

J.4832

1M9398-3 D/d.8803 10000 11/39 RP

This is the official death certificate the War Office issued, the date would have been noted by Fred and crossed referenced to the date of Aubrey's last aerogram. Fred would have realised the fact that he was in good spirits just a day before he was killed, and had no idea how the intensity of the air attacks had been building up over the week before the invasion.

The letter is dated 26th November, 1941 over six months from Aubrey's death, the wheels of officialdom work slowly. The family would have drawn little comfort in knowing the date of death, for all they knew he was still alive on the 2nd June, the full extent of the withdrawal would not be known to them until after the war when Prisoners of War living locally were repatriated, and those surviving members of 234 Battery who were posted on to other units were gradually demobilised.

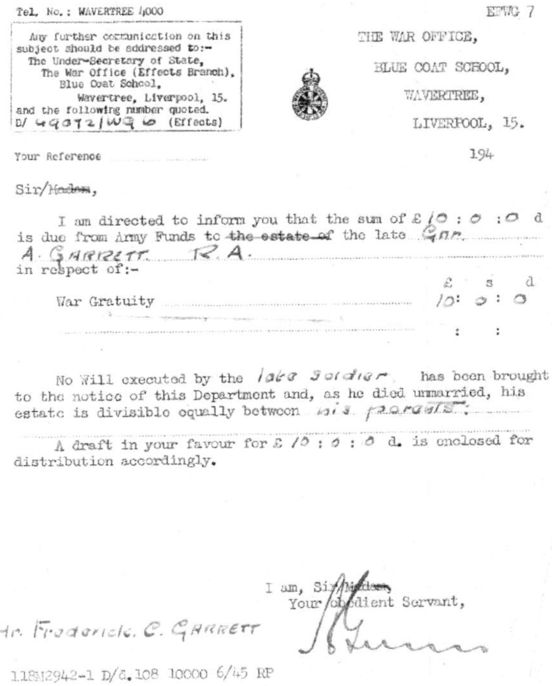

Tel. No.: WAVERTREE 4000

EFWG 7

Any further communication on this subject should be addressed to:- The Under-Secretary of State, The War Office (Effects Branch), Blue Coat School, Wavertree, Liverpool, 15. and the following number quoted. D/ 449372/WQ6 (Effects)

THE WAR OFFICE,
BLUE COAT SCHOOL,
WAVERTREE,
LIVERPOOL, 15.

Your Reference

194

Sir/~~Madam~~,

I am directed to inform you that the sum of £10 : 0 : 0 d is due from Army Funds to ~~the estate of~~ the late Gnr. A. Garrett R.A. in respect of:-

	£	s	d
War Gratuity	10	0	0

No Will executed by the late soldier has been brought to the notice of this Department and, as he died unmarried, his estate is divisible equally between his parents.

A draft in your favour for £10 : 0 : 0 d. is enclosed for distribution accordingly.

I am, Sir/~~Madam~~,
Your obedient Servant,

Mr. Frederick C. Garrett

118M2942-1 D/d.108 10000 6/45 RP

This was a death grant from the War Office payable to the next of kin, it was on a sliding scale with a private soldiers' family receiving ten pounds and a Corporals family receiving fourteen pounds[4] etc. Small comfort for the family, I am sure.

EFFECTS FORM NO.213.

Any further communication
on this subject should be
addressed to:-
The Under-Secretary of State for War
and quote D49072 Effects.

THE WAR OFFICE,

BLUE COAT SCHOOL,

WAVERTREE,

LIVERPOOL, 15.

14 JAN 1942

Sir/~~Madam~~,

I am directed to inform you that the sum of £15: 1 : 7 d. is due from Army Funds to the estate of the late No. 866845 Gnr Aubrey Garrett. R.A. ———— in respect of balance of pay and allowances.

No Will executed by the late soldier has been brought to the notice of this Department and as he died unmarried, his estate is divisible equally between the parents.

A draft in your favour for £7 : 10 : 10 d. is enclosed, together with a draft for £7 : 10 : 9 d. in favour of Mrs R.E Garrett.

I am,

Sir/~~Madam~~,

Your obedient Servant,

[illegible]

Mr F.C. Garrett
Myrtle Cottage
Bramling
Wingham.
Nr Canterbury.
Kent.

When the pay records finally caught up with 89 HAA Regiment, they would have worked out how much pay and oversees allowance would be due to Aubrey's family, together with all the others who had been killed, a form would have been sent to the War Office to distribute the funds accordingly, this was now the 14th January 1942, eight months after his death.

BUCKINGHAM PALACE

The Queen and I offer you our heartfelt sympathy in your great sorrow.

We pray that your country's gratitude for a life so nobly given in its service may bring you some measure of consolation.

George R.I.

I am unable to find a date for this letter from King George V1, I must assume it would have still been in late 1941. I am certain the signature is original and not a reproduction, so the King probably signed it himself. Some feat given the time it takes for correspondence; he would have signed many of these each day when time allowed.

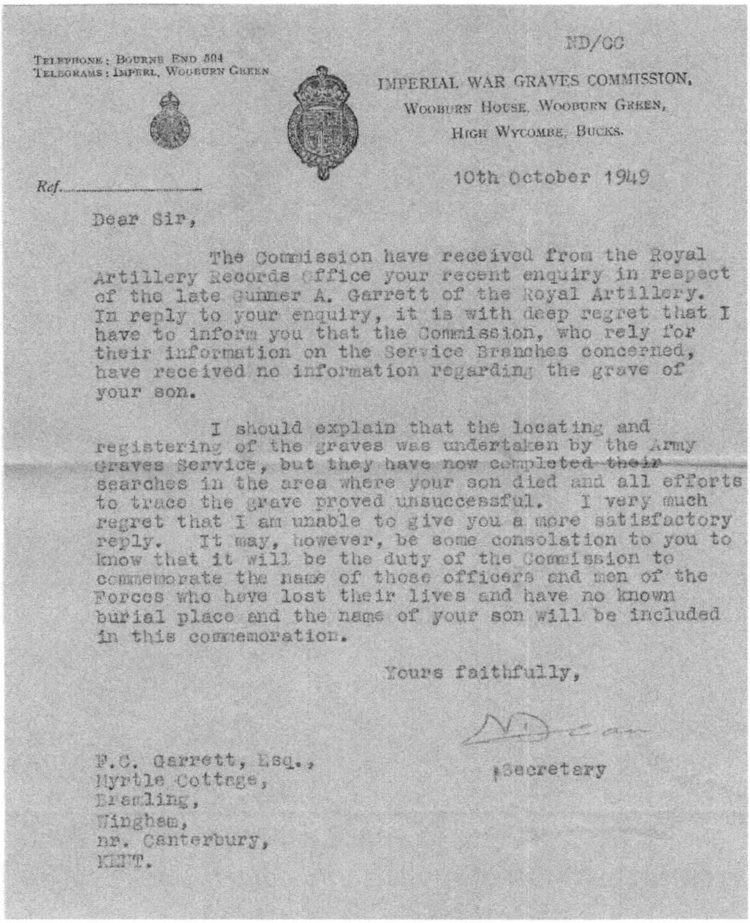

ND/CC

TELEPHONE: BOURNE END 504
TELEGRAMS: IMPERL, WOOBURN GREEN

IMPERIAL WAR GRAVES COMMISSION,
WOOBURN HOUSE, WOOBURN GREEN,
HIGH WYCOMBE, BUCKS.

Ref.

10th October 1949

Dear Sir,

The Commission have received from the Royal Artillery Records Office your recent enquiry in respect of the late Gunner A. Garrett of the Royal Artillery. In reply to your enquiry, it is with deep regret that I have to inform you that the Commission, who rely for their information on the Service Branches concerned, have received no information regarding the grave of your son.

I should explain that the locating and registering of the graves was undertaken by the Army Graves Service, but they have now ~~completed their~~ searches in the area where your son died and all efforts to trace the grave proved unsuccessful. I very much regret that I am unable to give you a more satisfactory reply. It may, however, be some consolation to you to know that it will be the duty of the Commission to commemorate the name of those officers and men of the Forces who have lost their lives and have no known burial place and the name of your son will be included in this commemoration.

Yours faithfully,

N. Dean

Secretary

F.C. Garrett, Esq.,
Myrtle Cottage,
Bramling,
Wingham,
nr. Canterbury,
KENT.

This letter would have been a real disappointment for Fred and Rose, they had hoped that a grave would be found and tended accordingly, the reality was the dead in Right troop were covered over in the trenches where they fell and left for a few years, in 1944 the Germans made efforts to exhume and reinterred centrally. At that point identifying the bodies would have been impossible.

They were eventually moved to the Imperial War Graves Commission site at Suda Bay, with the grave stones marked 'Known Unto God'. In reality the numbers don't add

up so there could still be bodies underneath the olive grove but we will never know.
The search for Aubrey Garrett would have been a long journey for his family, England to Crete nowadays is a four hour flight, just after the war it was impossible to get there other than by sea with several stops and boat changes.

Fred could never go and conduct a search for his son himself, I believe that he thought the War Office had not done enough to find Aubrey, he had made the assumption that he was in an obscure area with a rustic grave marker, missed by the system.

This of course we know to be untrue now, the Imperial War Graves Commission undertook an extensive search for bodies over three years to find those missing, the majority are now in the Suda Bay cemetery.

Fred carried the doubt with him for the rest of his life, the family always spoke about Aubrey during my formative years in a really positive way, almost with reverence, it seemed he was a legend of his time and sorely missed by all the family.

Aubrey was one of thousands who gave his life in the defence of good against evil, one young lad of many to whom we have the utmost respect, allowing us to have the life of freedom we enjoy today.

Epilogue

Now this book is completed, I have considered how long I have been on the trail to find Aubrey. Thinking back, it was probably when I could understand what the conversations and stories in the family meant. My Grandfather saw his son in me every day, we lived across the road and every stage of my development mirrored how he saw his son some thirty years earlier, which triggered the memories of that fateful day in 1941 when the telegram arrived.

I mentally stored the conversations and eventually, when my cousin passed away leaving me some of the family photographs, letters and documents. This completed the family archive and provided me with an insight of what happened during those times.

That said, the documents and subsequent research revealed a vast number of inconsistences, the stories repeated over and over by my family were mostly inaccurate yes, some truth but having done extensive research from many sources recently, it transpires that either the stories were embellished or Aubrey kept his own council on some of the important details.

Regardless of this The Letters provide a different and personal view on the tumultuous times at the beginning of the Second World War. Yes, the subject has been covered many times by a multitude of authors and publications, but I believe my story explains how the world appeared and played out for a 20 year old lad from Folkestone, it seems he was having fun and making the most of his time in the army sometimes oblivious to the bigger picture.

I feel for his parents at home with being bombed out in successive wars, living in subsistence conditions in a small hamlet several miles from civilisation. Aubrey must have been in every waking thought and with deteriorating health, Fred would have been in a very dark place indeed.

Fred wrote furiously to all branches of the War Department asking for details of Aubrey's grave, this continued until 1949 when he was informed that Aubrey finally had no known grave. The details of the Athens Memorial and a booklet were sent to the family with a copy of the commemoration photograph. Finally, Fred was able to begin to come to terms with his loss.

When my mother was nearing the end of her life in hospital, she asked me to go to Crete and try and find her brother. I willingly accepted the challenge and eventually we had a holiday on the island. I honestly didn't know where to start with my quest, the resort we stayed in was to the west of Maleme and the Tavronites bridge where so much happened during the first week of the invasion.

I laid a wooded cross on an unmarked grave in the Suda bay Commonwealth war graves site. I chose an unmarked grave as a symbol of the 49 soldiers from Aubrey's unit who were not identified.

After hours of research from War Diaries, written recollections, together with oral histories, I concluded that I should return to Crete and look at the area where Aubrey was based. The olive grove shown in the photographs was the gun site where the soldiers were killed. Immediately I felt a connection to the place, a sense of peace and tranquillity descended, a gentle warm breeze started and washed over me.

I was standing a couple of hundred yards from a busy highway but it was inaudible, I immediately thought about the possibility that all the bodies had not been found, there is a discrepancy of 3 in the total figures, I wondered if there was a slim chance, I was nearer to my uncle Aubrey than ever before?

We will never know but a sense of wellbeing purveyed through my world and brought to closure 80 odd years of family history. Where would we be today if Aubrey hadn't been chosen to transfer to 234 Battery? He would have gone to Sheffield or Derby with 223 and lived to an old age, married, had a family and worked his whole life for the Gasworks, who knows? His legacy lives on in this book and the letters and artifacts left behind by the family. He is commemorated on the war memorial in Ickham Church

Appendix 1 – Summary of Lt C Sutton's account of the invasion extracted from the War Diary of 89 Regiment October 1941

'Lt.C.E.B Sutton. Left Troop.

We disembarked at Suda Bay on Thursday, 24th April at 0600 hours. We marched from the docks to an olive grove in 42nd street and dispersed under the trees awaiting transport to take us to our gun positions.

At 1400 hours we were taken to Suda peak, and took over the 4 gun positions previously occupied by 151st Hy A.A Battery RA 700 feet above sea level. We had a commanding view of Suda bay from the south side, and we could fire a protective barrage over the quay and channel. We were attached to the 52nd Light A.A Battery RA. Commanded by LT.Col.Mather. R.A. 151st.Hy.A.A Battery were very helpful and gave every assistance.

The M.T. ship arrived on Friday 25th. April. We collected our guns and instruments and were ready for action at 0900 hours, Saturday 26th April. Sandbags were available, but the abundance of rock and stone made a suitable substitute.

We were immediately in action, reconnaissance planes being our chief targets. These were followed by dive bombing attacks on the quay and shipping anchored in the bay. For those attacks J.U.88s were mainly used, escorted by M.E.109s which also carried bombs and joined the attack. From now onwards we were almost continually in action, snatching short rest periods between action and vital gun maintenance. Food was not plentiful, Bully, biscuits and tea being the main ration. Later we received M&V ration and erratic supplies of bread.

Reconnaissance planes came over at regular times every day at 0700,1000,1200,1400 and 1600 hours. The main bombing attacks were always preceded by single planes at 10 to 15 thousand feet., obviously to draw fire and the enemy invariably used the sun for diving and attacking.

On the 11th,12th and 13th May we had night actions, DO17s at 8 to 10 thousand feet being the main target.

The searchlights picked up well. Following their high level bombing, the enemy machine gunned down the beams in a vain effort to try and escape the accurate and determined beams of the searchlights. We fired about 100 rounds each night.

During this time we prepared an alternative position 600 yards East, which we occupied on Wednesday 14th May. This position still gave us full protection over the quay, but improved our position to engage minelaying craft in the channel. By this time action was almost continuous, the quay and shipping being the main objectives.

On Friday 16th May a large force attacked the quay. JU's 87, DO's17, ME109 and JU88 dived in great numbers on the shipping and three ships were hit.

On Sunday this was repeated. It was apparent that each day brought more planes and the attacks and raids became almost continuous

The detachments did splendid work. Sgts Drayson and Carter worked tirelessly at gun control. They fought with great determination taking on close divers and scoring several direct hits. Many gunners suffered from deafness for days. All Command post personnel did magnificently, and the Lewis gunners and the men manning the .5" Multi-Vickers, faced up to the low flying attacks with great courage, with little cover they engaged all close targets and divers, and at least one plane was credited to them. The drivers handled their vehicles extremely well over roads and gradients often one in two. Our casualties for vehicles were nil (A good record)

On Tuesday 20th May the main attack was launched. J.U.52 gliders and parachute troops dropped in great numbers in the area of Canea. Maleme aerodrome was used to land J.U 52, troops, food supplies and arms. At 0700 hours S1 site at Canea was attacked with great determination. The position was bombed, then dive bombed by J.U87s and machine gunned by M.E 100s and 109 for about 30 minutes. The ammunition dump was hit and there were some casualties. Eventually the site was retaken by the Marines. At 20.00 hours we sent an officer and 20 men to clear up the site and brought back 32 survivors, instruments and two guns.

On Wednesday 21st May we were continuously in action, two 1.000lb bombs were dropped near the command post: only one detonated and caused a few casualties.

That night the detachments returned to our original position. Here we engaged J.U.87 who were strafing indiscriminately the gun positions, and dive bombing and patrolling the town of Canea. The detachments were getting very tired.

On Tuesday 27th May at 0700 we received orders to destroy our guns, instruments and transport.

At 0800 hours we evacuated and were told to march South near to Stilos, we were ordered to disperse in the olive groves and move only at night. Even then were bombed and machine gunned, receiving more casualties. We moved in small parties and marched through the night trying to complete the 35 miles across the island before Thursday night. We eventually reached the beach at 0100 hours on Friday the 30th and were taken aboard H.M.S Glengore and landed at Alexandria.

Appendix 2 – Summary of the battle by Lt A Corbett reproduced from the War Diary of 89 Regiment RA October 1941

Lt. A Corbett, Right Troop Commander

I was Right Troop Commander and G.P.O. on duty on the 20th. May, the day the German Invasion commenced.

The gun site was approximately 2.500 yds. Due south of Canea and 4.500 yds. due west of Suda docks. As it was proved by later events, the enemy had decided to land parachute troops around the village of Calatos about 3000 yards west of the gun site. All the time we had been in action, the troop's shooting had been most accurate, securing many hits and I am of the opinion that the enemy must have considered the guns as likely to cause considerable casualties to their troop-carrying aircraft, and in view of this the enemy's plan was to silence these guns.

At about 0730 hours we received a warning from G.O.R. of groups of aircraft approaching from the North and North West. The first to come into sight were several groups of D.Os 17 and 215 at varying heights and indiscriminate bombing.

These groups were engaged in quick succession. Then a large group of J.U.87 appeared flying level, towards Suda in the North East. These were engaged at height control and one plane was shot in half. During this engagement, spotters reported J.U.87s to the West. Before the guns (they were facing due East) could be traversed round eight or ten J.U.87 dive bombed the position from the West. This attack caused several casualties from splinters, but no direct hits on the guns. One bomb unfortunately hit one of the dispersed ammunition dump. The bombs and exploding ammunition caused a tremendous amount of dust. I sent for the medical orderlies to remove casualties, but within a minute or two of the bombing attacks, spotters warned me of low flying aircraft, and M.E.109s machine gunned and cannoned the site and our encampment nearby, for about six or seven minutes – these were engaged by L.M.Gs.

Peering over the sandbags with Milner, one of the spotters, through the dust we saw gliders all around the position. They landed near the command post before I had given the orders for close target.

The enemy from the gliders stalked the L.M.G posts one of which engaged the complete personnel of one glider.

All rifles in the command post opened fire immediately but we only had eight rifles on the site; four being left for the protection of the wagon lines.

The Lewis guns were in sandbagged emplacements and in turn the Germans stalked them and silenced them with hand grenades in the pits. Grenades were also thrown in the gun pits at the same time. During this period, we were keeping up rifle fire from the command post causing some casualties. At the same time, the Germans were using a small Trench Mortar from behind a hedge about 150 yards range. They were aiming at the command post; one shell falling inside causing many casualties, including poor old Peter (Lt. Stebbings) who had been doing valiant work with a rifle until then.

Eventually the enemy got into three of the gun pits and continued throwing hand grenades, trying to drop them into the command post. These grenades were small and round and seemed to burst after about 4 seconds. They have not a very effective burst in the open, but are quite effective in an enclosed space.

By this time, we had only two rifles going (Gnr Lawrence and myself). After getting one or two as they popped their heads up throw grenades, they started throwing blind from behand the sandbags.

Eventually I could see that practically everyone were casualties. I was hit myself and we decided to surrender. This was accepted by the Germans and the remaining few of us came out in the open. As we did so, Lt Cocollis and two telephonists came out with hands upheld yet were shot down in cold blood with a tommy gun. The same fate would probably been the fate of the remainder, had not the Boche who did it, wounded one of his own men. We were all taken prisoner and Nazi flags were laid out around the gun site. My slightly wounded men were made to bring in the dead and wounded, but were not allowed to bring ours in. They were then allowed to go to one of our tents and lie down. Later in the day, Marines re-captured the site.

When the Germans took the site, they placed a small charge of explosive in the breech of the gun, but this did not do a lot of damage except having a corrosive effect. They did not know much about their job as the instruments were not touched. Sometime in the evening I was removed to hospital.

The gliders were large cabin type, streamlined with metal skids under the fuselage with a very large wingspan. Each appeared to have about eight men. One carried a portable radio set, receiving and transmitting set, and one small mortar, about 3" calibre I should think and the remainder medium weight machine guns. Each man had a tommy gun and a revolver, two large satchels of hand grenades, each holding about 30 grenades, and one satchel of tommy gun ammunition and magazines. All were dressed in field grey uniforms. There were at least three officers, two of whom we wounded.

If we had sufficient wire to wire the position and all personnel were issued with weapons, this catastrophe could not have happened.

The noise of the bombs, exploding ammunition and the roar of the low flying aircraft made it difficult to get the orders through.

Appendix 3 - Capture on the Island of Crete excerpt from John Maynard's account of the capture and subsequent imprisonment.

John Maynard's account of the last few days of the invasion, capture and captivity on Crete. Reproduced with the kind permission of John's daughter, Mrs Patricia Young.

I arrived on the island of Crete at the end of April 1941 having come from Egypt on the ship, Ulster Prince, which incidentally was sunk soon afterwards off Greece. On arriving at the dock in Suda Bay my unit disembarked and we marched at least three miles finishing up in an olive grove, there to await orders regarding our final destination. After a meal of biscuits and tea we rested for an hour or so, lying about on the grass for we were rather weary. Soon I heard aircraft overhead, these proved to be five Italian Savoia bombers. Harmlessly dropping their bombs they were driven off by the A.A. defences. Once again we moved off finally reaching our position on the A.A. gun site 700-800 feet above sea level overlooking Suda Bay. Before going further I will mention that I belonged to a heavy A.A. Battery R.A.

The view from our position was rather lovely. Looking around I saw stretches of green fields, flowers, and in the rear, mountains faintly capped with snow. Looking down on Suda Bay and out across the blue waters of the Mediterranean it was a beautiful sight. Little did I think as I stood there then that this lovely scene was soon to be a place of hideous battle.

In the afternoon a flight of German J.U.88 paid a visit, chiefly to bomb shipping in the bay. The ships were hit and the planes then did some machine-gunning round about. I was forced to take cover behind a clump of stones as one plane played on our position. We could do nothing as our guns had not arrived from the dockside. Night came, we gunners turning to kip in our dug-outs, these being made by the Battery occupying this position before us. The morning arrived and passed without incident. During the afternoon our guns arrived and these were soon in action amidst some swearing and hard work. The remainder of the day passed quietly, we busying ourselves cleaning, oiling our guns, etc. The following morning we saw a little action with a German plane.

So, events led up to the attack and invasion of the Island. Prior to the invasion I will state briefly my work during the end of April to the first two weeks of May. During the day I was mainly engaged in cleaning guns, making a decent gun-pit, tidying up, all for the making of a tidy and soldierly place. The time I had to myself was spent in writing home, laughing and making enjoyment as best we could amongst ourselves. I never went further than our positions as orders forbade it unless special permission was given. So, of Crete itself I saw little until the evacuation and my misfortune to be taken a prisoner of war.

So, I come to the Battle of Crete. The week preceding this we all noticed the increased aerial attacks, both in number and ever-increasing strength. Targets at first were the shipping in Suda Bay. J.U. 87's (dive bombers) played a great part in this. Several ships were hit, some sank, others caught fire, some were saved, others were left to burn. One boat I shall always remember, an ammunition transporter. This received a direct hit, catching fire and finally blowing up in two amidst vivid flames, smoke and terrific explosions. The enemy's foremost idea at first, to my idea at any rate, was to paralyse our shipping going to or in the harbour thus cutting off supplies to our forces. This they failed in though not completely. Suda Bay was the only good place to unload and this place was a ship's graveyard during the day owing to enemy aircraft. So came the invasion by air born troops. We of the A.A. defences had already had a grim battle with the Luftwaffe but to this it was nothing. The 'Blitz', as we soldiers termed it, began with at least 75% of the German Air Force thrown against us night and day.

On Tuesday 20th May, 1941, the enemy attacked with huge numbers of bombers and fighters. These bombed and strafed everything they could. The right troop of my Battery suffered a great deal. Following the bombers came Junkers 52's (troop carriers), the troops coming down by parachute in hundreds but were quickly dealt with by our troops. Some landed on the site of the troops I just mentioned causing great havoc finally capturing the place. Many of my comrades were killed, others wounded, some lined up like dogs and shot down. Our troops recaptured the site soon; the troops taking part were the Royal Marines and the King's Royal Rifle Corp. At Heraklion and Malamy every parachutist was accounted for. Throughout the day wave after wave of bombers came, tons upon tons of bombs were dropped. Parachutists were still coming down as well, but the first day of the attack ended completely in our favour.

Next day the attack continued more fiercely, with this came the dreaded Stukas (dive bombers), their sole objective was to smash A.A. sites. To those who have never seen these machines operate, just a word. Their course is to fly over the target and then down on it in lightening dives. This dive is a great feat, the plane comes down vertically with ear-splitting and unnerving screams. So, when squadrons of these dive on an object you can imagine the terrific noise. All day they bombed A.A. sites, several of these were silenced during the day, many others as time passed. So accurate and deadly were their attacks that the A.A. fire greatly decreased; soon the enemy's planes could fly without serious fire from the A.A. Our site received its lot, twice we changed positions being bombed and strafed by machine guns each time. Two heavy calibre bombs landed amongst us one afternoon putting us out of action till early the next morning. Two days later we were again subjected to a dive-bombing attack but with our own fire drove them off with slight damage to ourselves. On the same day, in the afternoon, we were attacked by a low flying fighter, an M.E.109, the Spitfire of the Germans. This gave us a warm time for a little while. No-one was hurt but I had one bullet pass across the top of my shoulder through my shirt without much damage. So, we, the A.A. defences who were left, received hammerings day after day, more guns being silenced each day, the crews firing bravely to the end. My Troop was the last heavy site still in action, some 3" remained and Bofor (light AA) guns. With hardly any opposition from the ground the planes flew unhindered, more troops were dropped. Malamy aerodrome was captured. The bombing continued. The little town of Canea was reduced to ruins amidst which were the dead of hundreds of women and children. The Germans had established a defence now on the ground, these they tried to reinforce from the sea but were stopped by the Royal Navy who sunk about thirty ships out of the convoy.

More men dropped from the air closed in on the Galatas area and a fierce struggle started, the Mairi's (New Zealanders) finally clearing it with a terrific bayonet charge in which the enemy lost a great number of men. At the finish the enemy however got enough men on Crete to make a stand in which our Infantry were forced to retire. Not because of these enemy troops but by the overwhelming air attacks, for remember we had not the support of one British plane since the battle started. As the AA was not strong enough to do much damage now, German planes had their own way.

So, to the evacuation of the Suda Bay area. On the night of May 25th 1941, the last news we heard was that all was well in hand and the enemy was retiring. This seemed good to us who were all but done in after *nearly a week's continued action, firing our guns for hour after hour. So, we turned in for the night, had a few hours' sleep, but were soon banging away again. Imagine our surprise when about 07:30 our Battery commander, Major Hukins, came and informed us we were evacuating the island. Or rather in his words we were to withdraw from our present positions. He explained we should have gone at 02:00; the news should have been sent through by a Royal Marine Unit some distance from us. It never came though; the Marines simply left at 02:00 leaving us without passing the orders on, so we were 5 hours behind in starting. Things began to hustle; enemy aircraft were already overhead doing their deeds. The orders were then given to blow up our guns which we did much to my regret as an artillery man and pride for my gun. Thus, we set off for Sfakia on the south of the island, a march across Crete, no roads except rough stone tracks mostly.*

Ten minutes after leaving our site about thirty dive bombers attacked it, evidently thinking we were still there. Had we have been there many of us would have been killed or wounded. For an hour or so my comrades and I marched over rocks and hills finally being forced to take cover under an olive grove as aerial activity was fierce. Sheltering beneath the trees were other men, chaps from different Regiments and four or five of my own Battery, a total of about one hundred. Here we lay talking and smoking for a little while in peace though planes were roaring about overhead. Soon however, through some of the chaps running about carelessly, we were spotted. A Royal Marine Officer drew his revolver threatening the next man who ran about a bullet. So having been found we expected some bombs or machine gunning; it came firstly by a Junker 88, screaming downwards it let go a salvo of death, whistling through the air and tearing into the ground all around us with terrific explosions. A second lot followed, one of these dropped about twenty feet from where my comrades and I were lying, a blinding flash, ear-splitting detonation and whistling of shrapnel, the bombs being anti-personnel one. Screams and groans of pain filled my ears, at least twenty men or so had been hit, including four of my comrades. I dashed about doing what I could for them, it was rather difficult as the planes were machine gunning from the air relentlessly. I dodged to and fro anyhow, got to one of my pals, Taffy Jones, who had received a shell splinter over the right eye and the bottom of his back. I made him as comfortable as I could but he died soon afterwards, so I lost one of my best comrades and friends. My two other pals, Craycraft and Whorlow, had both been wounded. Craycraft had some slight wounds in his shoulders; Whorlow a nasty wound in his rear quarters. I did what I could to ease them, gave them some water out of my bottle. Lying next to Craycraft was a young chap out of a light

AA Battery, his face blown away; he was still alive and able to speak a little. He asked for some water which I gave him. I put a shell dressing over his face as best I could, made him comfortable and sat down amongst my dead and wounded comrades. One other chap from our Battery was killed there, Sgt Linkstead, a very nice fellow. So, I remained there until nearly sunset, doing little services of comfort to my fellowman as best I could. At sunset my remaining pal and I moved off having been told by one officer to do so, telling us that ambulances would be soon be along to collect the wounded. By now they had been lying there six hours or more without any treatment as none was available. Never shall I forget that day out of all the horrors I have witnessed.

So, my pal, Jim Gower, and I walked, or rather stumbled, on down slopes of rock, through valleys and up slopes again. This we did for about an hour when a squadron of dive-bombers came over. These began to play havoc on a small village nearby, bombing and machine gunning furiously. We lay and watched this scene until it was over and off, we went again. Soon darkness fell and after another hour's trudging we struck a rough road full of troops marching to our place of evacuation. Mingled with these were women and children, both young and old, with their few belongings in a bundle on their backs. Some were crying and shouting, all struggling along, a pitiful scene. All through the night we carried on, resting now and again. All the food we had with us was two tins of corned beef. We ate one, this being the first meal for nearly twenty-four hours. We also drank some water from our bottles. We then set off finally stopping at dawn for a little sleep, but no sooner had we done so when we heard the old familiar drone in the sky. "Aircraft" I said to my pal. They passed over our heads quite low looking for signs of moving men; that was the last we saw of that flight.

After a couple of hours, we again moved, moving cautiously, always alert for planes - to be seen was deadly not only for ourselves but to our other comrades who were somewhere around. The day passed quite peacefully for us, occasional planes now and again. By now we had eaten our supply of food except for a tin of emergency ration chocolate which we kept until we were forced to eat it through sheer hunger. All day we struggled on, by 7pm we came to a valley place packed with troops by the hundreds. Here parties of fifty were being formed and taken over by an officer if possible. My pal and I got into one of these and moved off, led by a Major. We tramped on until somewhere about midnight when we were held up, the road being packed with men in front and rear. In the front the men were being checked by two officers in charge of embarkation. This cheered us up as we thought we were near the beach and would embark that night. However, by the time we reached the officers we were told that no more man could pass to the beach as the ships had to be away and out to sea by dawn for fear of enemy planes. So very disappointed we broke up and looked for somewhere to sleep. My pal and I stumbled over some rocks finally finding a cave-like arrangement where we lay down and were soon asleep, two hungry chaps, tired and weary caring little at the time about what would become of us.

We were awakened in the morning to the sound of aircraft, a couple of enemy fighters, ME 109, were flying around and around, looking for signs of men. They evidently found some further away for we heard series of machine-gun bursts. The bullets from these planes are deadly for they explode on impact, making a terrible wound on a body, nearly always fatal if they hit. Things quietened down and we lay still in our cave. Towards midday we heard voices below us several hundred feet down the mountain side. To me one of those voices seemed familiar so we hailed them three or four times. My surmise proved right, the voice I thought I knew was that of one of our officers, Lt. Horton, and a few of the boys. So, we clambered down to where they were resting, slipping on stones, dislodging rocks that hurtled down the mountain into the ravine below. Reaching our fellow men we rested, talking over different ways to the beach. Finally, we decided to move so the party climbed down the remaining dangerous slope to the ravine. Once at the bottom we felt safe as to our side rose cheer cliffs of rock and mountains, the latter studded with pines. We had a long rest beneath the rocks, overhanging in places. We were all terribly hungry having had nothing to eat for three whole days; worse than that was the terrible thirst, far more agonising than hunger. Water on Crete is supplied by wells which are few and far between, about half a dozen in each little village, very primitive wells at that. After an hour we set off along the ravine, a sorry looking party. My feet were a mass of blisters by now. I could hardly walk, the pain was awful, so I just stumbled on behind with my pal beside me. The pal I shall never forget. We shared everything at all times in England, Egypt, everywhere we went, right up to our first four months as prisoners when we parted. Anyhow for several miles we trudged on, finally we smelt and saw the sea and a small Cretan village away on the right, hoping with the few drachmas we had to buy bread or something from the villagers. In this we were unlucky, there was nothing to be had as many other troops had passed by and they had received all the villagers could spare. We did however find a well whose water was greenish in colour but our thirst was so intense we greedily drank our fill. Four days or more had elapsed since we had eaten so you can guess our state of health. Continually walking, hardly any sleep, unwashed and unshaven we made a sorry picture to behold. We again moved on reaching the vicinity of Sfakia our embarking point towards night. The ravine and surrounding places, such as caves and areas under trees, were filled with men, the number totalling thousands. Some had been there two days or more having been lucky having been lucky in obtaining vehicles and getting there more quickly. Night came so we expected some at least would embark when the ships came under the cover of darkness. Word came through that no men could be taken off as the Navy could not manage it as they were engaged elsewhere. This carried on for a couple of nights but all men were confident of being taken off in the end.

Each day that passed brought its aerial activity. Sfakia was attacked repeatedly and bombed. The last of May brought a flight of fighters towards the evening wreaking havoc with their machine guns. A lot of the men were nearly mad with the incessant attacks from the air. The battle in the hills between our rearguard action and the oncoming enemy infantry drew nearer and we knew our men were retiring to the beach for a last stand. Also, they had been strengthened by two battalions of Commandos (shock raiding troops) from Alexandria. It was of no avail, do not forget though as far as enemy troops were concerned, we had them beat. It was the air which beat us, the enemy was supported to the full by its air force while we had none. So came the fateful day of June 1st. The first action of the day came from an enemy mortar section that poured their shells over for a while but did hardly any damage at all as they had not got the correct range. At almost 10am there was a terrific roar of engines in the air and overcame waves of enemy bombers. Their intention was to bomb the ravine and neighbourhood. If this attack had come hundreds would have been killed as escape was impossible trapped in the bottom of the ravine. After an hour imagine our horror when we were informed by a senior office that we were prisoners of war; our rearguard had no alternative but to surrender as it was impossible to evacuate any more men as the ships couldn't come. All were horror stricken, an army left to its fate without any help being afforded.

From the start organisation was nil, through inefficient officers, an army making its way anyhow, anyway, as best it could. On learning he was a prisoner a young Australian next to me drew his revolver and shot himself through the head, dying instantaneously. We threw down our arms, steel helmets, respirators and awaited our lot. Through some difficulty or error, a few enemy fighters still continued strafing, killing many men, including one or two of their own. Soon our captors appeared in our sector, a few men of a Bavarian Alpine regiment. We were rounded up, there seemed millions of us, troops everywhere, we looked a pitiful sight. I myself had not eaten for nearly six days, living on foul well water. At being gathered more or less together we were allowed to sit or lie down until things were found out where we were to go to. A lot of us were lying about in an old churchyard, I myself was for one. Whilst there, someone started to play a piano accordion, the first tune he played was "I'll Pray for You". That tune with its lovely words nearly brought tears to my eyes. I felt an ache around my heart. So, the day wore on, at about 5pm we were roused up, starting to march down the ravine, up over the mountain side onto rough stone roads, common in Crete. I could hardly walk, my feet were one mass of blisters, my strength half gone. There were hundreds like me. Some dropped completely exhausted, some never to rise again. The long line of men seemed endless, plodding wearily as best we could. We carried on until nightfall, being turned into a field like cattle for the night. We sank to the ground all utterly exhausted and were soon asleep.

In the morning we were roused as soon as it was light and started off once more. We trudged all morning until midday when we came to a small village. Here the Germans gave us a packet of biscuits and a tin of bully between three men; the food was our own captured by the enemy. This was very welcome as I had not eaten for nearly a week. In the village I stopped an old Cretan and asked if he had any Krassi (strong Crete wine). He said yes and I asked him to bring some if he could without the Germans seeing him. He came back with a small stone jar holding about half a gallon. For this I gave him one hundred drachmas. My pal and I had a good drink of this wine saving some for later on. We felt a new life come into us after drinking that wine. Within another hour we were on our way once more, the last lap of our march to Canea. I could not make much progress as my feet were giving me terrible pain, blistered, burning and aching. On the way we managed to obtain water at several points from different wells. Thirst was my greatest trouble, far worse than the hunger. So, we go on, we passed the spot where my comrades were killed a few days previous; they still lay where they had died. Pitiful sights too after having lain for over a week in the hot Mediterranean sun, flies crawling over them, the smell was awful.

We walked past on towards Suda along by the bay we had looked down on so often, then through the village of Suda on to Canea. The inhabitants of the village tried to give us food only to be roughly handled by our guards. A lot of islanders had suffered terribly at the enemy's hand already, many being shot. We passed through the town of Canea, now a mass of ruins having been bombed unmercifully. Many women and children lay buried beneath debris, innocent victims of cowardly, deliberate bombing raids. We reached our camp, or rather an open space of sands near the sea, where previously hospital tents had stood, these the parachutists had destroyed the first day of the invasion. About five thousand of us were dumped in No. 3 camp as it became known to us. There was nothing in it just a stretch of sand down to the sea. Here we slept, laid and done everything, our bed the earth and the sky our covering. It was summer time so not cold. Here we received one meal a day, a small cup of dirty soup consisting of some kind of greyish lentils, just enough to keep us going. Soon many men were attacked by dysentery, some died, others were left weak and practically helpless. No medical attention and things were as bad as they could be. So, things were, the hot summer days made it worse. At night we just lay down on the ground in our overcoats, those who had them at any rate.

After a fortnight of this I managed to get on a working party at Galatas, may comrade as well. Our job was far from pleasant, digging up and reburying the dead, mostly Germans, a few English. We dug trenches six feet deep, about twenty long and just dropped them in, throwing the earth back as we went along. For this we received a loaf of bread and a tin of bully a day, a big thing to us in our present state. This lasted two to three weeks. Back in camp things were still the same, thousands of hungry, dirty looking men, more like animals than men. Twice I escaped with my pal from the camp to look for food only to be forced back. I could have stayed out altogether hiding out in the mountains aided by the inhabitants. I thought of my people at home though. We should be sent to Germany sometime and would be able to communicate to home. If I stayed out hiding, I would be left behind and my people would know nothing of me. So, things carried on, men living under the worst possible conditions, treated like animals.

Today as I look back to our early days of captivity, I wonder how we survived it. Several of the men in the camp were given punishments in public before the Cretans for little things like laughing at the guards. After six weeks of this we left for Suda Bay one morning at 4am. We were crammed into the holds of a small ship like cattle. In the afternoon we left arriving two days later at Salonica. Here we were herded into the old Greek barracks. Here we lived far worse than before. We couldn't move without a burst of machine gun fire.
So, I close this story as I only intend writing of Crete. What I have written is true and my own experiences.

Photographs

Gunner Aubrey Charles Winter Garrett

Bennett/Garrett family archive

Traditionally all recruits and transferees had a head and shoulders photograph taken on joining a Regiment. Aubrey's photograph still exists.

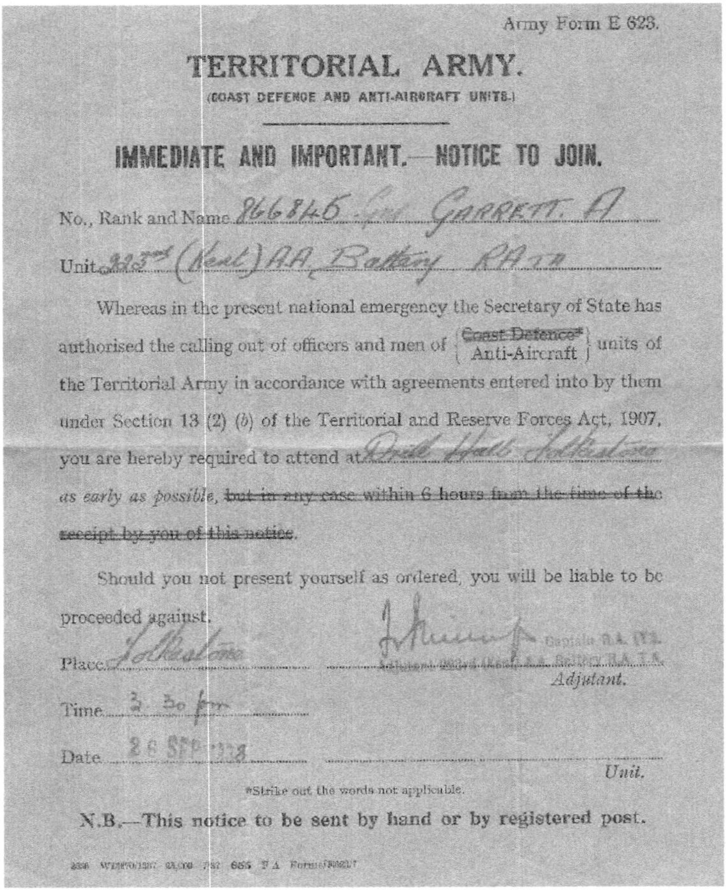

Army Form E 623.

TERRITORIAL ARMY.

(COAST DEFENCE AND ANTI-AIRCRAFT UNITS.)

IMMEDIATE AND IMPORTANT.—NOTICE TO JOIN.

No., Rank and Name 866846 Gnr Garrett A

Unit 223rd (Kent) AA Battery RA TA

Whereas in the present national emergency the Secretary of State has authorised the calling out of officers and men of ~~Coast Defence*~~ Anti-Aircraft units of the Territorial Army in accordance with agreements entered into by them under Section 13 (2) (*b*) of the Territorial and Reserve Forces Act, 1907, you are hereby required to attend at Drill Hall Folkestone *as early as possible*, ~~but in any case within 6 hours from the time of the receipt by you of this notice~~.

Should you not present yourself as ordered, you will be liable to be proceeded against.

Place Folkestone

Captain R.A. (T.A.) Adjutant 223rd (Kent) A.A. Battery R.A. T.A.

Adjutant.

Time 3.30 pm

Date 26 SEP 1938

Unit.

*Strike out the words not applicable.

N.B.—This notice to be sent by hand or by registered post.

This was the form sent to Aubrey to be called up for the month on, month off, I understand they were stood down in the middle of October 1938 when the threat was perceived to be an overreaction.

Photo courtesy of the Bennett/Garrett family archive used with the kind position of Gerry Warren, editor of KM Group (initially taken by the Folkestone Herald)

Soldiers reporting after call out at the Shellons Street Drill Hall, awaiting orders. Aubrey Garrett is in the front rank fourth from the right. Out of view I suspect is an NCO or officer is explaining what happens next, as the faces of the men show they are absorbing the orders/information being given.

Bennett/Garrett family archive

223 Battery at camp in Watchet 1938, Aubrey is looking at the camera, front rank 7th from the right. The troop appear to have been photographed during a rest period, happy faces clearly have a bit of fun, as soldiers this would have been at someone else's expense, such is the gallows humour of soldiers worldwide!

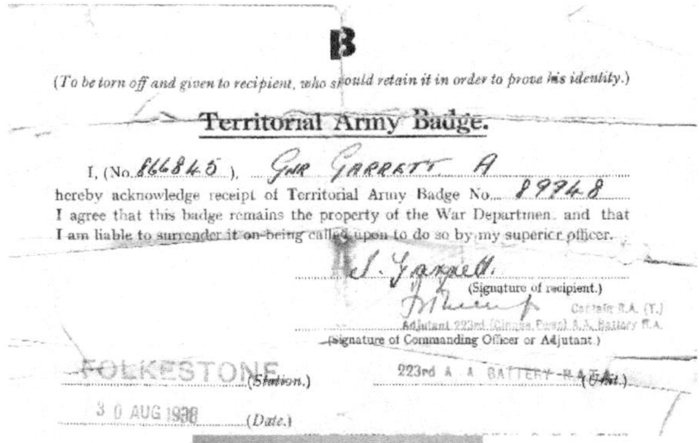

B

(To be torn off and given to recipient, who should retain it in order to prove his identity.)

Territorial Army Badge.

I, (No. 866845), Gnr Garrett A

hereby acknowledge receipt of Territorial Army Badge No. 89748

I agree that this badge remains the property of the War Departmen and that I am liable to surrender it on being called upon to do so by my superior officer.

S. Garrett.
(Signature of recipient.)

Captain R.A. (T.)
Adjutant 223rd (Cinque Ports) A.A. Battery R.A.
(Signature of Commanding Officer or Adjutant.)

FOLKESTONE (Station.)   223rd A A BATTERY R.A.T.A. (Unit.)

30 AUG 1938 (Date.)

Photo credit John Bennett

All TA soldiers once they had completed their training were awarded a TA lapel badge up until around 1980, they were made of white metal and numbered on reverse. Aubrey's badge is not within the family anymore, its whereabouts is unknown despite a trawl around various collector.

Photo credit John Bennett

This is the camera Aubrey took everywhere with him. It is a Kodak folding Brownie 2 model A, still quite common in camera circles owned by collectors, they are still available for about 25 pounds. In 1940 the price new in the US would have been one Dollar, (equivalent to $33 in 2023). Aubrey would have either bought it second hand or been given it by one of his more affluent relatives. As part of the rules for travelling oversees the camera would have been left with his parents in September 1940 with a partly exposed film inside.

Photo credit John Bennett

This print is from the camera, it was developed in 2023 some 83 years after the photograph was taken. Max from Canterbury Cameras suggests it is a figure wearing a helmet.

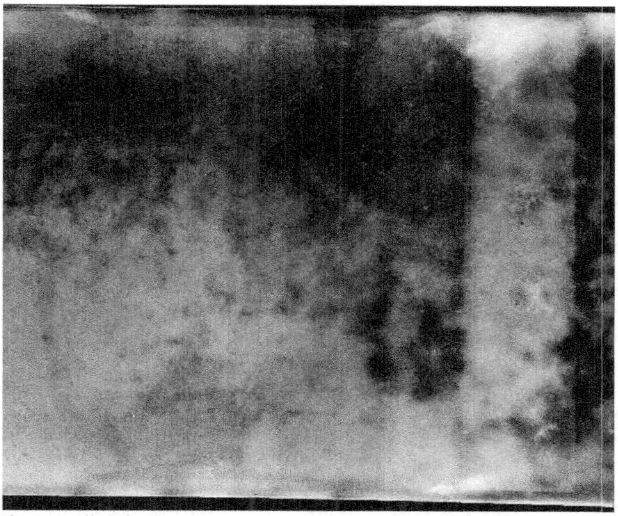

Photo credit John Bennett

This is the second photograph from Aubrey's camera, there may be a figure standing in rear of shot?

Photo courtesy of the Bennett/Garrett archive, originally taken by the Dover Express

On the 10th of April King George VI visited the guns sites in Dover, He visited D2 with the gunners 'at action' he is seen in this photograph with Colonel Sadler CO of 75th Regiment and his staff officer entourage. Aubrey Garrett standing with the gun as indicated.

Photo courtesy of the Bennett/Garrett/Newing archive.

This is a photograph of Butlins Holiday Camp in Clacton just after WW2, it remains unchanged from the time Aubrey was there. This aerial view it looks like a typical army training camp, so very little needed to be done in terms of accommodation changes to host troops preparing for operations.

Photo from Bennett/Garrett family archive

Photo of Aubrey (left) with an unknown friend, on leave from TA camp in Minehead. Note the swagger sticks they carry, these were issued so they didn't walk around with their hands in their pockets. When you carried them, you had to tuck the stick one under your left armpit and hold the tip whilst marching along in a military fashion swinging the other arm. They have been in use since the 1800s to prevent soldiers out of camp looking scruffy! They are also wearing jodhpurs and high puttees, from the time Aubrey signed on and the unit was still field artillery pulled by horses.

Image courtesy of the Bennett/Garrett archive

This is the Christmas card Aubrey sent to his parents just before he went to Egypt, simple and to the point.

Bennett/Garrett family archive

This photograph was taken during leave with four of his friends, Aubrey is second from the right, his friend Albert Ward is far right, the others are unknown at the time of writing.

This was a staged photo taken by a professional photographer, if you look on the floor next to Albert the number 17 is shown clearly, this would have used to identify groups of soldiers to sell the correct ones to the unit for onward transmission to the soldiers themselves.

The Pyramids are four miles from Cairo in 1941, accessed by a single lane track carved into the desert, today in 2023 the city has grown almost up to the pyramids themselves. The photo below was taken in 2019 from the Pizza Hut restaurant now just across the road!

Photo courtesy of Sean Doherty

A company of Home Guard which includes many employees of the Folkestone Gas Company. In the centre is Mr. G. E. R. Diamond, recently appointed Manager of a gas undertaking in North Kent.

Press cutting from the Garrett/Bennett family archive

The Home Guard platoon from the Gasworks, Aubrey would have worked with, and known everyone in this photograph. This press cutting together with the article about Wally Cooper was posted to Aubrey and went all the way to Egypt and back again in the envelope stamped deceased.

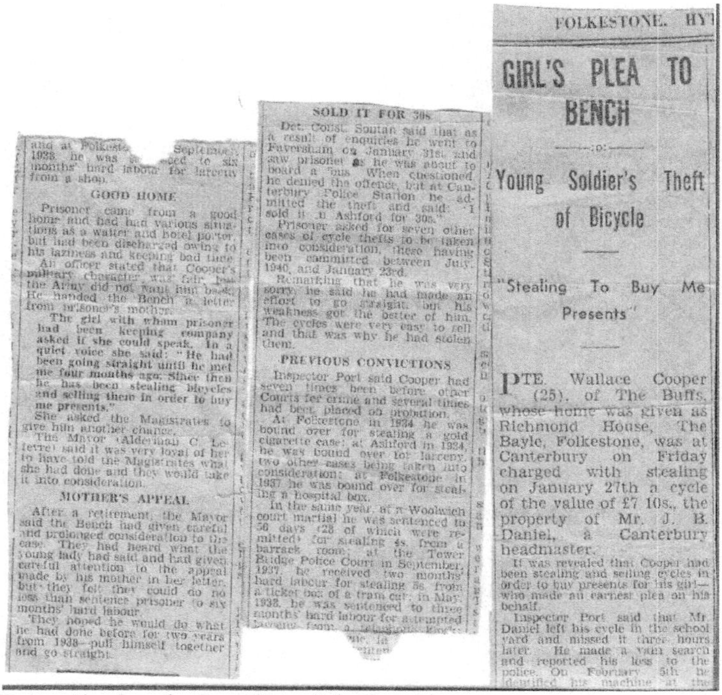

FOLKESTONE. HY[illegible]

GIRL'S PLEA TO BENCH

—:o:—

Young Soldier's Theft of Bicycle

"Stealing To Buy Me Presents"

PTE. Wallace Cooper (25), of The Buffs, whose home was given as Richmond House, The Bayle, Folkestone, was at Canterbury on Friday charged with stealing on January 27th a cycle of the value of £7 10s., the property of Mr. J. B. Daniel, a Canterbury headmaster.

It was revealed that Cooper had been stealing and selling cycles in order to buy presents for his girl—who made an earnest plea on his behalf.

Inspector Port said that Mr. Daniel left his cycle in the school yard and missed it three hours later. He made a vain search and reported his loss to the police. On February 5th he identified his machine at the

SOLD IT FOR 30s.

Det. Const. Soutan said that as a result of enquiries he went to Faversham on January 31st and saw prisoner as he was about to board a 'bus. When questioned he denied the offence, but at Canterbury Police Station he admitted the theft and said: "I sold it in Ashford for 30s."

Prisoner asked for seven other cases of cycle thefts to be taken into consideration, these having been committed between July, 1940, and January 23rd.

Remarking that he was very sorry, he said he had made an effort to go straight, but his weakness got the better of him. The cycles were very easy to sell and that was why he had stolen them.

PREVIOUS CONVICTIONS

Inspector Port said Cooper had seven times been before other Courts for crime and several times had been placed on probation.

At Folkestone in 1934 he was bound over for stealing a gold cigarette case; at Ashford in 1934, he was bound over for larceny, two other cases being taken into consideration; at Folkestone in 1937 he was bound over for stealing a hospital box.

In the same year, at a Woolwich court martial he was sentenced to 56 days (28 of which were remitted) for stealing 4s. from a barrack room; at the Tower Bridge Police Court in September, 1937, he received two months' hard labour for stealing 5s. from a ticket box of a tram car; in May, 1938, he was sentenced to three months' hard labour for attempted [illegible]

and at Folkest[illegible] September, 1938, he was [illegible]ced to six months' hard labour for larceny from a shop.

GOOD HOME

Prisoner came from a good home and had had various situations as a waiter and hotel porter, but had been discharged owing to his laziness and keeping bad time.

An officer stated that Cooper's military character was fair, but the Army did not want him back. He handed the Bench a letter from prisoner's mother.

The girl with whom prisoner had been keeping company asked if she could speak. In a quiet voice she said: "He had been going straight until he met me four months ago. Since then he has been stealing bicycles and selling them in order to buy me presents."

She asked the Magistrates to give him another chance.

The Mayor (Alderman C. Lefevre) said it was very loyal of her to have told the Magistrates what she had done and they would take it into consideration.

MOTHER'S APPEAL

After a retirement, the Mayor said the Bench had given careful and prolonged consideration to the case. They had heard what the young lady had said and had given careful attention to the appeal made by his mother in her letter, but they felt they could do no less than sentence prisoner to six months' hard labour.

They hoped he would do what he had done before for two years from 1938—pull himself together and go straight.

Press cutting from the Garrett/Bennett family archive

This press cutting was cut out carefully and posted off to Aubrey, it explains the Court appearance of his friend Wally Cooper who Fred would like to have seen kept better company, hopefully Wally would have learnt from the errors of his ways after this sentence and gone on to lead a sensible and fulfilled life. This press cutting travelled half way round the world and then back again as undelivered!

Photo John Bennett

In 1940 this was the field where the gliders landed. The area shown is approximately where the Command post was located where Aubrey was killed. Nothing remains of the battle today as everything has been absorbed into farmland.

Photo John F Bennett, taken by Rikki Jenkins

The author to the west of the gun position, the four gun pits would have been in a horseshoe pattern to the rear of this picture.

Photo John Bennett

This fence marks the northern boundary of the right troop position, the furthest gun pit would have been a few metres inside this fence. A memorial 234 Battery, Royal British Legion cross positioned by the author on March 2023

Photo John F Bennett

The Left troop gun position high on the cliffs overlooking the bay, 151 Battery positions (John Maynard's account) would have been on the hills to the left of the small island.

Photo courtesy of The Imperial War Graves (in the Bennett/Garrett family archive)

The unveiling of the Athens memorial for those killed in the Greek Campaigns, dignitaries and military representatives, a copy of this photo was sent to the families of the deceased, together with a book containing the names.

Photo courtesy of Doug (Buster) Beckett

The memorial as it is today, standing out as a fitting place to remember all service people killed in the Greek Campaign. This photo was taken from the position of the wreaths in the photo above.

Photograph taken by John Bennett

Aubrey's medals L to R, Battle of Britain, Africa Star and War Medal. He didn't qualify for the Defence medal as you had to survive the entire war and have served 180 days. The Greek Campaign medal from the Greek Government was applied for in November 2022, in November 2023 an invitation to attend an awards ceremony at the Greek Embassy in London arrived, the author attended an exclusive ceremony on 20th December the photograph of the award is below together with the medal and commemorative certificate.

Official photo courtesy of the Hellenic republic Embassy London

His Excellency Ioannis Tsaousis presenting the medal and certificate to the author at the Greek Embassy in London. All recipients are now 'Friends of the Greek Embassy' in recognition of their ancestor's contribution to the defence of Greece in the second world war.

Translated into English the certificate reads Greek Republic, 1940 – 1941 campaigns commemorative medal. We Award Gunner Garrett, Aubrey Charles 866845. Who took part in military operations 1940 – 1941. Signed by Minister of Defence Georgios S D Nikolaos and certified official by Teorgios Bosinas Brigadier General.

The UK Medals Office issued medals for Aubrey's service during 1946, he received the War Medal and the Battle of Britain Star. The author realised after they came into his possession that he had not been awarded the Africa star, he applied and in due course was advised he hadn't served in Egypt! This didn't ring true and after some research covered elsewhere, Aubrey had in fact spent over a month in Egypt.

A copy of his service records was annotated accordingly, a copy of them and a letter finally produced a brand-new Africa Star and a certificate seven years after first trying to apply and seventy-seven years after the initial qualification.

References

Chapter 1

1. Details on the withdrawal from France extracted from WO 167/717 held at the National Archives at Kew.
2. The Royal Artillery archive at Larkhill provided a summary of 223 Battery designations and weapon configuration for the period mentioned.
3. Information taken from IWM histories, Basil Grose, a radar technician posted to Swingate noted the officers were still wearing breeches and carrying riding crops, even after the fiercest engagements, looking completely out of place. He commented on the fact they were obvious pre-war TA, completely out of touch!
4. 234 Field Battery TA was split to form a new Battery, 234 Battery (HAA) with its headquarters at Deal Kent, 223 Battery (HAA) continued to be based at Folkestone. The Government identified that a likely attack would come from the air, so plans were put in place to increase the air defence capability along the South coast. Information from Wikipedia and Aubrey's service record.
5. On 2nd April 1916 an accident happened at the ammunition depot at Uplees near Faversham, 108 people were killed in the subsequent blast and fire, researched from The Great Explosion published by Penguin books and Kent County Council's Exploring Kent's past. 2nd Lt H Stebbings of the $2^{nd}/3^{rd}$ RFA led a party of rescuers into the area assisting with the recovery of survivors, extinguishing the fire and removal of bodies. 2Lt Stebbings was awarded the Edward Medal for which

he had to wait until 1918 because of the protocols of awards not in the face of the enemy.

6. The Emergency Powers (Defence Act) act of 1938 was used to mobilise reservists and Territorial soldiers for specific periods, generally speaking the home defence anti-aircraft units were mobilised for month on month off but sometimes this was shorted to 3 weeks if the situation allowed. This was initially deemed a 6-month situation and after stand down everyone who mobilised received a £20 bounty. The bounty is a matter for conjecture, some documents state it was just £5 The staggered call out meant that soldiers could still work in their normal employment.
7. Details confirming the use of Queen Bees was confirmed in the book Harvest of Messerschmitt's by Denis Knight ISBN 9780723227724 sadly no longer in print, this book outlines the use of DH 82B Queen Bees and together with information from the De Havilland Museum provides a casual look at this tiny aircraft.
8. The historical significance of this speech has been debated over the years and many believe this was the moment that the country finally with much sadness, knew there was to be another war. BBC archive.
9. Fred's grandmother passed away after a short illness probably brought on by the stress of their home and shop being damaged by a lone bomb dropped by a Zeppelin. After trying to sort out the mess of the stock and damage Fred decided to sign on full time and walk away through sheer frustration. There were many relatives who would have been due a settlement but despite letters to the War Office to release Fred to come home and sort out the mess, he didn't complete the task until 1919. Hell in My Head John F Bennett ISBN978183780875.

Chapter 2

1. Hell in My Head, Fred was taken from the front line to play football for the army, every time he returned all friends had been killed, this had an adverse effect on his state of mind.
2. The 223 Battery war diary WO 166/2248 confirms the date of full time call out.
3. Both German and English aerial photographs show the white rings around the tents and gun pits, they were clearly a target from now on.
4. Details confirmed in A Fury of Guns by Peter Erwood, ISBN 0907322727 Published by Arcturus press, Peter was in 233 Battery for the early stages of the war.
5. After the expansion of units with cloning and new Regiments formed from scratch, Queen Bees were highly sought after, getting them local to the unit must have been a bonus, sadly there was so much red tape that the Battery on the cliffs never saw them to train with. Harvest of Messerschmitt's by Denis Knight ISBN 9780723227724 refers to the chaos at Hawkinge where everyone seems to have been based in short order.
6. Swingate was a WW1 airfield with its claim to fame as the airfield used to refuel biplanes before their hop across the channel in 1914. It consisted of a few huts along the runway, by 1940 it had expanded almost down to St Margarets Bay, a distance of nearly a mile, and almost a half mile deep. A significant target but essential to keep the hundreds of troops near to their places of works. Some estimates suggest that there was nearly two thousand troops based at Swingate. This did not include 75th Regimental headquarters who were based at the old prison above Dover docks.

7. In 1940 a study was conducted by the British Medical Association into the efficacy of the injections, it was published on the 5th November 1940 in the medical journal Hansard.
8. On the 14th May 1940 Winston Churchill broadcast to the nation to join a new force for home defence, it was named the Local Defence Volunteers, thousands of WW1 veterans joined together with teenagers too young to serve in the regular forces. The government were expecting around 150 thousand but within a month there were 750 thousand signed up for the force. This of course meant the uniforms and weapons were in short supply, many soldiers paraded carrying pitchforks and homemade weapons, looking like something from the Middle Ages. On 23rd August the name was changed to Home Guard. There were more than a million men in the Home Guard up until the stand down in December 1945 Source https://www.home-guard.org.uk/hg/history.html
9. Operation Pied Piper was the working name for the evacuation of children from assumed dangerous towns in 1939, approximately 150,000 were evacuated, in 1940 following Dunkirk a further 100,00 were evacuated from vulnerable towns on the south coast. Dennis Garrett was part of this latter tranche. https://www.bbc.co.uk/history/british/britain_wwtwo/evacuees_01.shtml and IWM.
10. When the retreating soldiers of the British Expeditionary force finally arrived at Dunkirk plans were being made to evacuate them from the small port. This would have taken far too long and caused a bottleneck; the beach was shallow and destroyers and naval vessels could not get close enough to lift the soldiers in significant numbers. Operation dynamo was the name given to the task.

To overcome the beach draught the government Ministry of shipping requisitioned 850 small boats with a shallow draught from various sources, many privately owned along the river Thames. Between the 27th May and the 4th June, they helped to lift 336,000 British, French and other allied soldiers to safety. Some acting as a shuttle going back and forward to the beaches several times a day. Ever since these boats have become known as The Little Ships of Dunkirk. Source The Little Ships of Dunkirk Association.

11. Source WO 167/717.
12. 3 Division dug in and held off the German advance for several days around the perimeter of Dunkirk before surrendering when news of the evacuation numbers was communicated. They were running low on ammunition and food, and the Navy decided it was too risky to try and remove them from the beaches as the Germans by then had complete air superiority.
13. 51 Division War Diary.
14. Territorial Officers in the 1930s would not have seen regular attachments, their experience of war was based on training manuals and hearsay. Those who has served in the first war were by now quite senior in rank and post touch with the basics of war fighting. In 1918 a second lieutenant had his tactics based on the mood of the time, warfare had evolved into what we know today as All Arms warfare, Infantry worked with the Airforce and Navy and Infantry worked with Tank, Engineer and Artillery closely to ensure all aspects of the operation is coordinated.
15. The Royal Society for the Protection of Birds maintains checks on Migratory birds to judge the population at any given time. The pathway between the bases of the huts on D2 is aligned perfectly for

this task, the nets are strung out on frames approximately ten feet from the ground on fibreglass poles. They are checked every morning and the captured birds are weighed, health checked and finally tagged so their progress can be traced if caught again.

16. During the Peninsular War soldiers only had one uniform issued by their Regimental Colonel. This was designed for temperate climate, but when soldiers deployed abroad, they had to hope they were ging to a cool climate. The rules were you couldn't take off your jacket unless off duty, so all tasks such as digging had to be done in full tunic. Very hot in Spain and Portugal for the Peninsular campaign in the summer, but spare a thought for the soldiers defending the British interests in the Caribbean.
17. Doug Cullen is commemorated on the Brookwood 1939-1945 memorial, Panel 5 Column 3.
18. Operation Sea Lion was the code name for the invasion of Great Britain, in the build-up of this the Germans amassed a huge flotilla of landing craft in the channel ports ready for the operation to begin. As soon as it was cancelled the landing craft were taken away from the ports.
19. Dates obtained from the RAFA website and verified by the Bentley Priory Museum website. The dates are officially 10th July to 31st October, some pilots of the time would have challenged this fact as they were making many sorties well before and well after!
20. The IWM histories have copies online but as far as I can surmise, no paper copies exist locally.
21. There are myths and misconception regarding the apparent snubbing of Jesse Owens by Adolf Hitler but none of this is true. The press wanted to make something of the German Aryan Warrior myth so fabricated the whole story for sensationalism. Hitler

did not shake hands with Owens but nor did he congratulate anyone else on that day either, he had been reprimanded by the Olympic committee for showing favouritism to his own team so he declined to congratulate any winners. Details courtesy of History News Networks. Jesse Owens was the most successful athlete of the 1936 games.

22. The Women's Auxiliary Air Force was established in June 1939 and mobilised for full time service in August 1940, finally disbanded in 1949 when serving women were absorbed into the RAF as the Women's Royal Air Force. At its peak there were 182000 serving WAAF's. Details confirmed by the RAF Museum Hendon.
23. Information gleaned from Robert Hall and his research, the Royal Marines History website/archive, White Cliffs and Dover Museum.
24. The Government realised that civilians should be compensated for loss or damage to their houses and property and in 1943 The War Damage Act was passed. Set amounts for the loss of homes and fixings was introduced, the scheme was managed by the local council but essentially it was unfair to the owners of properties in wealthier areas. For instance, the value of a three bedroom terraced house in Liverpool, was definitely worth far less in an affluent area of Folkestone! Obtained from Hansard May 1941.
25. Fortunately, there are enthusiasts who specialise in the history of the East Kent Road Car Company, I am indebted to Richard Wallace, historian and expert on all thing's buses. Richard still has timetable information from all those years ago.
26. Double Summertime was imposed gradually, the clocks didn't return to GMT in October 1940 instead stayed as they were. In April 1941 they went forward

an hour where they remained for the remainder of the war. This made the best use of daylight.

Chapter 3

1. The Squadrons based at Bekesbourne were No2 Squadron for a few weeks, and for two days No 13 Squadron. The airfield was closed in 1939 and reactivated in 1940 for just a few months. It was closed on 8th June 1940. The airfield was then covered in dug in spikes to deter it from being used as a landing zone for German aircraft or parachutists.
2. Morris Gun Tractors were built for the sole purpose of towing artillery pieces and their limbers. Their exact specification was Morris Commercial C8 FAT (Field Artillery Tractor) They were made in the Morris factory in the West Midlands, some 10,000 were made. The vehicle had a large engine for its size, a Morris 3.5 litre ideal for towing heavy guns and ammunition. It had a driver and could carry 5 crew in the rear compartment. The War Diary mentions that two of these had to be used in tandem to tow the guns up the mountain to get to the Left troop positions.
3. Post Traumatic Stress Disorder (PTSD) is a stress related mental health problem affecting service personnel, emergency services first responders and those that have witnessed trauma. These days its treatable but in 1941 there was no understanding of its causes and effects, just carry on as best as you can. Today it is so different, PTSD is a high focus in decision making in the military. See Hell in my Head by John F Bennett and for reference the Service Champions coursework notes for Kent, Medway and East Sussex Armed Forces network.

4. Cliffhanger, a Gunners story by LW Clark mentions this, the new predictors suddenly meant they hit less aircraft, it appears the calibration was not correct and specialist had to visit units tore calibrate them. Fortunately, the old Vickers Predictors were still in the Quartermasters stores ready for back loading. They were reissued very quickly.
5. Operation Sea Lion was the code name for the invasion of the British Isles, it was only feasible if the RAF was destroyed, and became the focus of the Luftwaffe in the previous few months. Changes of tactics, advances of radar always kept the British pilots one step ahead. In the end the Germans gave up and decided to hit the infrastructure to force civilians to rebel against the Government, this of course only strengthened the resolve of the British people. Peter Fleming – Operation Sea Lion ISBN 0-330-24211-3.
6. Ickham the Friendly village by Leonard C Coombs gives a full breakdown of the agricultural use of land in the area in early 1940.
7. From firsthand experience the orders process can be convoluted, the orders are received at Regiment level and broken down into tasks, operational, logistical and training needed to achieve the task, once a plan is set it is disseminated to individual batteries who break down the orders further. This effectively is down to troop level with individual responsibilities given out, ie transport, spare parts, ammunition, logistics, communication and rationing as an example. The reality of this would be not many soldiers below the rank of Corporal would have little idea how much background activity was going on, giving the impression of 'not much going on'.
8. Spare parts supply would be put on the highest priority, well above the other units based in the UK,

spare vehicle sparts, gun barrels, instruments, clothing, general equipment would be on a three day turnaround. Depending what was sitting in the Ordinance depots, most parts would arrive at Regiment within a few days, Batteries would receive their share and vehicle load lists produced. This would enable the QM to be able to find a specific part at a moment's notice.

9. Charles Garrett was a printer by trade, working in local printers and newspapers all his life in Folkestone. He and his wife Alice were bombed out of their home in 1940 and moved to Cambridgeshire, they rented a house in the country to get away from the war.

Chapter 4

1. The 'phoney war' had dragged on for months with no apparent escalation of hostilities, this action on the Altmark was heavily publicised by the Government to give the population a morale booster, at last the population could see something was actually happening.
2. Even before the war Brazil nuts were a rare delicacy, so to get a pound of them at Christmas was indeed a luxury, they had to be shipped from South America, not easy in time of war.
3. WO169-1583 the War Diary of 89 Regiment shows the port as Durban.
4. The Office for National Statistics (ONS) was the source for this.
5. Kelly's directory states the details about public houses in Folkestone at that time. Mackeson's' brewery must have taken an enormous financial hit with the sudden loss of sales.
6. BMA journal 1940.

7. Details handed down to me by my father, Fred Bennett plus verified by Hansard 1938.
8. Details confirmed by Hansard and BBC WW2 archive data.
9. Several references to Neurasthenia are found all relating to same causes and effects, Encyclopaedia Brittanica, various BMA journal articles, and the British Psychological Society.
10. Italy entered the war on June 10th 1940, the British authorities interned several thousand Egyptian/Italians men of working age, these were located in camps in the desert which Aubrey refers to. Reference Josef Lebovic Gallery.
11. I consider that the most likely place Aubrey was sent to was in the area of Ismailia, it had a large POW camp nearby so this was the most probable area.

    When people were called up and or volunteered, they were given serial numbers, although they had been accepted, they were not called forward until their number was due. This prevented huge numbers in the system which ultimately couldn't cope, this was a throwback to the first war when they took everyone with no thought of the logistics. Bill was given 37 as his serial and eagerly awaited his turn to go to training. The family always said Bill died far too early based on the stress caused when he was constantly being machine gunned, working to replace and adjust antennas on the roof of the listening station at Capel Le Ferne, he was always on edge and highly strung after his service. He was awarded the usual medals but they were never taken from the box, the paper and certificate are untouched. Recently the author has had them, together with Aubrey's and Gladys's medals mounted for posterity in a single frame.

Chapter 5

1. WO 169-1583 chronicles the build up and disposition of 234 Battery.
2. Corned beef in a tin was universally known as Bully Beef or just Bully, the biscuits were hard baked with minimum fat content to enable them to stay fresh. You could eat them as they were but this presented a danger to the teeth of the consumer, mostly they were softened with water to make a porridge substitute.
3. WO 169-1583 mentions this together with the firsthand account of Albert Glind, a gunner in Right troop (IWM audio history).
4. IWM audio interview with Albert Glind.
5. Albert Ward mentioned this to me back in 1997 when we lived nearby, also hearsay from my father Fred Bennett how knew one of the gunners who was in Right troop that day.
6. Charles Milner describes the day with great alacrity, and the visit in hospital from Colonel Stebbings, audio histories from IWM.
7. WO 169-1583-89 Lists the after-action reviews by Lt Sutton and Corbett, summarised as annexes to this book.

Chapter 6

1. One of the traits of someone who is a sufferer of PTSD is they become obsessive, the thought of losing a son was bad enough but Fred was focused on finding a grave that it became his obsession for many years. This started when the letters dried up as he knew that something was wrong.
2. It would have been after the soldiers returned from either Prisoner of War camps or released from their service engagements, would the family have any

knowledge of what happened that day. From what I deduce the facts regarding the actual death of Aubrey would have been withheld by his friends to save more upset for the family.

3. This was a bad day for the Gasworks, they would have lost a few of their employees that day I am certain.
4. Hansard May 1939.

Acknowledgments

I would like to thank Andrew Newsom for supplying the War Diaries of 4th Buffs, 89 Regiment RA and 234 Battery RA. They proved invaluable to verify the events and actions mentioned in the letters.

Callum Jackson for typing some of the letters when I tore my retina just at a crucial moment, without his help the project would still be in its infancy.

The IWM vocal histories.

Sian Mogridge, archivist at the Royal Artillery Archive C/O Artillery House, Royal Artillery Barracks, Larkhill, Wiltshire SP4 8QT, for providing confirmation of 223 Battery/75 Regiment's displacements during 1939/1940, and the National Archives at Kew for supplying the War Diaries.

Cara Jones for providing the oral history of Albert Glynn her grandfather, gunner with Right Troop 234 Battery.

Pat Young for the photos and the written account of her father, John Maynard from 151 Battery who shared the gun position with 234 on the hills around Suda bay, I have included his account in the text as a useful historical record. I believe it gives the reader a more rounded account on what happened in those chaotic days in May 1941.

Special thanks go to Andrew Morgan, volunteer for the National Trust who walked me around the D2 gun site on the cliffs above Dover. Although nothing remains of the original sandbagged emplacements, the site now has been unearthed revealing the concrete emplacements added in 1941 as a more permanent home for the anti-aircraft guns.

I would like to mention Robert Hall for the tour around the gun site at D2 and his extensive knowledge of the Battery. A copy of his book in progress Guns on the White Cliffs of Dover, had interesting information to allow me to cross check some of the facts. This information he gave freely which enabled me to build a picture of the time Aubrey spent at Dover in 1939/40.

The village archive of St Margarets Bay enabled me to view and confirm details from the book Cliffhanger – A Gunner's story by JW Clark, the diary from the perspective of a gunner stationed at D2 during the time I am researching. D Clark was a gunner in 223 Battery some 300 meters from the village, this gave me confirmation of dates and events in the Garrett/Bennett papers. Special thanks to Christine Waterman for facilitating this. The St Margarets Bay history society provided snippets which backed up the family history and local knowledge.

Rikki Jenkins my 'advance party' who lives on Crete has done a fabulous research job on the Left and Right troop positions, and the Monastery where the wounded were taken. Rikki spent time overlaying modern maps over the WW2 maps and through thorough detective work, found the exact position of Right Troops' position. On my brief visit to the island, he accompanied me and walked the positions. I offer my most sincere gratitude and thanks!

I would like to thank Max Lamdin of Canterbury Camera Centre who carefully removed the exposed film from Aubrey's camera, it had been lodged there since 1940 and the internal frame was corroded needing some careful prising open without damaging the delicate film inside.

A very special thanks to Mick Meakin who unravelled the responses from the Federal German Archives in Freiburg.

Doug (Buster) Beckett supplied the recent photograph of the Memorial in Greece plus additional information regarding the campaign.

Sarah Thomas assisted me in tracking down 'A Fury of Guns' the memoir of Peter Elwood, a gunner in 223 Battery RA who was on the cliffs with Aubrey, this book confirmed facts and assumptions. A dusty shelf in St Margarets library revealed the book. Ironically the library is barely 300 metres from the gun positions atop the cliffs where Aubrey was based.

Paul Markland for lending me the copy of Harvest of Messerschmitt's by Dennis Knight this book proved invaluable for research into the local area during 1940 and the anti-aircraft guns in the area.

Sarah Stevens nee Ward provided me with information about her father Albert Ward with whom Aubrey had served. I lived near Albert in Northbourne in the late 90s. Albert was captured on the Right troop gun site and spent the remainder of the war in POW camps. He must have been a free spirit as he finished his captivity in Colditz Castle, the secure facility for frequently escaping prisoners!

Albert hadn't spoken about the war to any of his family, but when I said that my uncle was in his unit, his demeanour changed and he told me many things about that time. He said he was with my uncle when he was killed but didn't elaborate. Sadly, I should have written down his story then.

Following on from my visit to Crete in March 2023 I discovered that one of Aubrey's fellow gunners had only recently passed away, Alf Hey was captured and was a POW for four years. I have spoken extensively to his son, Bob Hey to cross check information and compare notes.

Brian Dengate for the background information regarding the B17 bomber who he witnessed crashing as a child.

Richard Wallace for his extensive knowledge on the historic details for the East Kent Road Car Company.

My wife Sue for hours of patience and support given while this book was in its infancy.

Fiona Doherty for her editing skills and keen eye for detail…

Who's who!

People mentioned in The Letters and a brief description of their role etc.

Frederick (Fred) Garrett – authors Grandfather, had a successful antique shop in Folkestone until it was destroyed by a random bomb from a Zeppelin in WW1, he joined up and saw action on the Western Front. He sustained shell shock, what today is deemed post-traumatic stress disorder which became worse as he became older.

Rose Garrett – authors Grandmother nee Newing, Wife of Fred Garrett, sister to Fred, John, Charlie Pheobe, Harry and Syd Newing.

Gladys Casey – Frederick Garrett's sister lived in Folkestone across the road from the Garretts until the mid 1930's Her husband died in the flu epidemic in 1919 and was a single parent.

Raymond Casey – Son of Gladys Casey, was treated like a brother by the Garrett family spending a great deal of time with then during their formative years. Raymond went on to be an eminent geologist having become an expert in fossils and sedimentary rocks found in the Warren along the coast from Folkestone.

Charles and Alice Garrett – parents of Fred Garrett and Gladys Casey, retired printer from Folkestone who moved to Lincolnshire after their house was destroyed by bombing.

Aubrey Garrett – eldest son of Fred and Rose Garrett about whom the book is written, born in 1920.

Frederick (Bill) Garrett – second child of Fred and Rose Garrett Born 1921, married Nellie Rolfe in early 1950s.

Gladys Garrett – only daughter and third child of Fred and Rose Garrett (mother of author) Born 1923, married Frederick Bennett 1951.

Dennis Garrett – youngest son of Fred and Rose Garrett Born 1928, unmarried, retired early from Air Traffic Control in the 1980s due to Multiple Sclerosis.

Granny – Granny Newing was the matriarch of the Newing family she had 15 children, Pheobe, Lily, Charlie, Syd, John and Harry all crop up in the letters. Harry gets a mention for his darts playing skills. The Newing family originally came from the Kentish village of Elham, they were mostly farm labourers in the local community.

Uncle Charlie – Charles Newing was a sufferer of what we know today as post traumatic stress disorder (PTSD). He suffered badly on the return from WW1 and spent most of his life in and out of the mental hospital in Chartham near Canterbury. He had a psychotic episode in 1939 and hid the family valuables including medals and silverware, in the woods in the middle of the night. They were never found. Rose Garrett's brother.

Uncle John – Edward John Newing lived with his parents and brother working on local farms, he also had mild PTSD having worked in a labour battalion in WW1. Rose Garrett's brother.

Harry (Henry) Newing – Rose Garretts brother, lived near Wingham in 1940.

Fred and Dolly Newing – Lived at Crocksyard, former gamekeeper for Lord Fitzwalter's estate heavy horseman for the farm at Crocksyard near Wingham.

Lilian (Lily) Newing- Only child of Fred and Dolly, believed to be disabled but no records exist of these only conversations with her aunt, my great aunt Pheobe who was Rose's younger sister. Pheobe was the last surviving Newing of that generation.

About the author

John Bennett was born in Canterbury and educated locally. He can count six generations of military in his family, mainly army but both his parents were in the RAF in WW2. In 1974 he joined the Royal Air Force to be trained as an aircraft mechanic. During the third week of basic training John together with several of his intake were asked to re-muster as firemen as they had over recruited. John decided to leave and joined the motor trade to train as a mechanic.

In 1978 he joined the Territorial Army, the Queen's Regiment which became the Princess of Wales's Royal Regiment, partly to assist in work progression and partly through curiosity as his uncle was in the TA in 1936 through to his sad death in 1941. It was through the memories of his mother and a vast number of photographs and letters that the interest in military matters was born.

In 1988 John left the motor trade and joined Sun Alliance insurance as a Staff Motor Engineer where he progressed via a convoluted route to become a team leader of motor engineers in the north of England, Scotland and Northern Ireland.

John took early retirement in 2013 and became involved with the Princess of Wales's Royal Regiment (PWRR) Regimental association, assisting with its growth and development. John is also passionate about the Regimental Museum in Dover Castle and worked as a volunteer assisting with outreach projects and doing talks and tours. John retired from this role in 2022.

John was also on the Regimental Heritage Committee representing the TA and Army reserve, retiring in 2023. In addition, John was the Mental Health Champion in the Regimental Association and is a qualified Mental Health first aider.

Printed in Great Britain
by Amazon

44261863R00119